LINCOLN CHRISTIAN COLLEGE AND SEMINARY

W9-BLX-386

The New Leviathan

> *Christianity must give its message to a world in which Leviathan in its different aspects threatens all human existence to its very roots.*
>
> PAUL J. TILLICH

By the same author

China's Real Revolution
The Spread of Christianity
The Story of Methodism
      (In collaboration with Halford E. Luccock)
World Revolution and Religion
What and Why in China
Storm Over Asia
The United States of Europe
The Ordeal of Western Religion
From Victory to Peace
    and others

The Earl Lectures for 1945

The New Leviathan

By PAUL HUTCHINSON

 1 9 4 6

WILLETT, CLARK & COMPANY
CHICAGO   NEW YORK

Copyright, 1946, by

PAUL HUTCHINSON

*All rights reserved, including
the right to reproduce this book
or portions thereof in any form.*

PRINTED IN THE UNITED STATES OF AMERICA

To
the memory of
JACOB BURCKHARDT
and
the inspiring friendship of
HARRIS FRANKLIN RALL

116406

FOREWORD

Many will ask, Why another book on the relations of church and state? There have been so many! Dr. M. Searle Bates, in his monumental volume on *Religious Liberty*, fills fourteen pages with bibliographical references in small type to available important books and magazine articles on that single aspect of the larger topic with which I am here attempting to deal. Haven't these books covered the ground? What reason can there be for another, especially in view of the fact that its author cannot pretend to the scholarly competence that marks many of the volumes on the church-and-state issue already available?

My only answer is that this issue has, within the last few years, taken on new forms, and that it comes to us today with a new exigency because of the rise of the modern totalitarian state. The threat of totalitarianism has not been ended by the downfall of fascist dictators in Europe or of the military state which so recently sought to rule Asia from Tokyo. It is a living, growing menace. I do not believe that the Christian churches, or their membership, have as yet awakened to the varied forms in which this menace threatens the future.

The essence of this totalitarian threat, as it presents itself in the Western democracies, lies in the increasing tendency to look to the state for the ordering of all of life and every life. In thus turning to the state, man is of course seeking security. But the cost is slavery.

Our contemporary trend toward totalitarianism does not always result from the state's lust for power. That is, to be sure, a factor to be reckoned with. But greater danger today arises out of the panic of the " little man " who has lost his nerve in a world that has become too grim for him to face. Where is he to find heart to face such a world unflinchingly, to reassert his claims to freedom and the rights which freedom bestows?

I believe that he will find in the Christian church, in the heritage of that Judeo-Christian prophetic message which has inspired so many struggles for freedom in centuries past, the reinforcement for mind and will he so desperately needs. And I believe he should be told so; that the church at this hour should be telling him so with a new urgency, clarity and boldness.

It happened that in the early months of 1945 I was invited to deliver four series of lectures on issues of contemporary church life. The first was a lectureship on " Religion and World Politics " at the University of Oregon, during the first week in February. The second was the annual Earl lectureship at the Pacific School of Religion, which was to be given at Berkeley during the first week in March. The third was before the annual Ministers' Institute at the University of Kansas City, in May. And the final series was to be given at Garrett Biblical Institute, in Evanston, Illinois, during June and July. I therefore determined to have all these lectures deal with the one central problem of the relation of the church to the totalitarian state — the modern Leviathan.

The result is in the reader's hands. The lectures are presented much as they were delivered, except that at a few points interpolations or expansions have been made in an effort to take into account the great events which took place between the delivery of the last lecture in mid-July and the delivery of the manuscript to the publishers.

In no sense can this claim to be a " last word " book. It is simply a fumbling and much too limited " first step " into a vast and perplexing subject. Of one thing, however, I am sure. The problem with which this book tries to deal is real. It is here. It is growing. And if Christian churchmen do not

recognize it and start to do something about it soon, they may
be too late. This group of lectures is sent out in this form,
therefore, with the hope that it may induce some of its readers
to do something. At the least, it may turn some minds into
new channels of thought.

P. H.

Winnetka, Illinois
October 1, 1945

CONTENTS

The New
Leviathan

CHAPTER I

The Resurrection of Thomas Hobbes

I

On January 30, 1649, at the order of a revolutionary tribunal, a London executioner cut off the head of the Most High and Mighty Prince, Charles the First, by the Grace of God King of Great Britain, France and Ireland, Defender of the Faith, and so forth. The headsman's axe dealt such a blow to the doctrine of the divine right of kings that eventually it was to disappear from the earth, except in Japan, where it seems fated to a not distant extinction, and in the remote recesses of Tibet. Two years after the death of Charles, the last rebellion against the power of the Commonwealth was broken at the battle of Worcester. And two years after that decisive battle — or, to be exact, on December 16, 1653 — Oliver Cromwell assumed the title of Protector of England.

But Cromwell, who had led a civil war in rebellion against a monarchical absolutism, maintained such a military absolutism of his own, purging and dismissing Parliaments at will and ruling by the naked power of his army, that after his death in 1658 the Commonwealth was quickly swept away and Charles II recalled from exile to a restored throne. However, it was not to the absolutism of his father and grandfather that Charles returned. Marston Moor and Naseby, Preston and Dunbar had not been fought to no end. Even the duplicity and tenacity of the Stuarts, as James II was presently to discover, could not deliver England back into the despotism of early Stuart days. Within thirty years after General Monk seated Charles II on the throne amid the extravagant transports of the people, the Habeas Corpus Act had been enacted to secure the liberty of the subject, the supremacy of Acts of Parliament over proclamations of the crown had been established, and England's monarch was reigning under the constitutional limitations imposed by the historic Declaration of Right of 1689.

This bit of historical background must be kept in mind if one is to perceive fully the significance of the appearance of a book which rightly finds its place among that chosen hundred on which Chancellor Robert Maynard Hutchins has placed his benediction as the books which have contributed most to the intellectual progress of man. For in the year 1651 — which is to say, halfway between the execution of Charles I and the ascension of Cromwell to the dignity of Protector — an Oxford don named Thomas Hobbes, moved, as he says, " by the disorders of the present time . . . to set before men's eyes the mutual relation between protection and obedience," published his *Leviathan, or the Matter, Form and Power of a Commonwealth Ecclesiastical and Civil.*

This striking title with its biblical overtones, as Hobbes tells us at the only place in the text where it is used (in Chapter XVII), mirrors his conception of the nature of the state. The state, according to Hobbes, reaches its perfection when all men have, by mutual consent, surrendered all authority to one ruler, " that great Leviathan, or rather, to speak more reverently, that *mortal God* [Hobbes italicizes this description of the state] to which we owe under the *immortal God* our peace and defense." Then Hobbes proceeds to paint this picture of what is, for him, the ideal state:

" By this authority, given him [that is, the absolute ruler] by every particular man in the commonwealth, he hath the use of so much power and strength conferred on him, that by terror thereof, he is enabled to perform the wills of them all, to peace at home, and mutual aid against their enemies abroad.

And in him consisteth the essence of the commonwealth; which, to define it, is *one person, of whose acts a great multitude, by mutual covenants with one another, have made themselves every one the author, to the end he may use the strength and means of them all, as he shall think expedient, for their peace and common defense.* And he that carrieth this person, is called SOVEREIGN, and said to have *sovereign power;* and every one besides, his SUBJECT." (From Chapter XVII, " Of the Causes, Generation and Definition of a Commonwealth.")

One would think that ideas of this sort as to the proper constitution of the state, published only two years after the execution of England's king, while the Parliament was still riding high, would have put Hobbes in peril of his life. Perhaps they did. Certainly he found it prudent to spend much of his time in exile in Paris until the Restoration. Yet even the downfall of the Commonwealth does not seem to have helped his popularity much. For though Charles II was under some personal obligation to him, since he had served as his tutor while that monarch was Prince of Wales, as a Stuart the king could hardly overlook the fact that Hobbes's theory of absolutism rested on the idea of a " social contract " — the idea, that is to say, that even absolute governments are constituted by the voluntary compacts of men who form them as a means of guarding their security. Hence it logically would follow, as even a Stuart could comprehend, that the same men who made the contract could dissolve it. So there are those who claim that Hobbes was quite as well satisfied with the strong-arm government of a Cromwell as of a Stuart; what he did *not* want was what he considered the chaos of parliamentary rule. Since he thus pleased neither side in the strife which covered England throughout his lifetime, the probabilities are that Hobbes would have made another in the select group of philosophers who have ended their days in prison or exile had he not found a haven of refuge in the bosom of the powerful Cavendish family, whose head, the Earl of Devonshire, knew and honored him as the tutor of his son.

There is a great temptation to linger with Hobbes's ideas of the origins of government — the "social contract" entered into by men in order to escape from the war of each against all others (*bellum omnium contra omnes*) which he held to be the nature of primitive existence, The "social contract" idea passed from Hobbes to John Locke, to Rousseau and his disciples, and finally to the men who wrote the American Declaration of Independence and made the French Revolution. But of more immediate concern for our study is Hobbes's other belief that the purpose of the state is to insure peace and security, and that this is to be achieved by placing in the hands of the state overwhelming power, unlimited authority; by making the state a great Leviathan — so great a Leviathan as to be a "mortal God." *The state as mortal God!* That was the vision of government vouchsafed to Thomas Hobbes amid the confusion and slaughter and panic of revolutionary England three hundred years ago. And that is the vision of government which some men — far too many men — see amid the confusion and slaughter and panic of these days.

To be sure, Thomas Hobbes was a philosopher without much honor in his own day. He lived in an inconspicuousness that was almost hiding, and he died at ninety-one almost unknown to his own countrymen. What little stir he had created as a political thinker was quickly forgotten in the acclaim given to John Locke and his ideas — ideas that Locke himself was to say had been formulated "to justify to the world the people of England" in their revolt against the Stuarts and absolutism in government. Locke picked up Hobbes's idea of a social contract, but Locke's social contract led to a government, not of unlimited, but of strictly limited, powers, and these never to be exercised in such a fashion as to deprive men of that life, liberty, property and pursuit of happiness which was their due under natural law. We are, of course, in large measure the heirs of this Lockian tradition, which found full expression in Thomas Jefferson and his dictum that " that government is best which governs least." The father of the American Revolution was not George Washington or Benjamin Franklin or even Samuel Adams; the true father of the American Revolution was John Locke, dead seventy-one years before Bunker Hill.

Today, however, the pendulum is swinging away from Locke and back toward Hobbes. Modern man is no longer so sure as were the men who signed the Declaration of Independence that liberty is the supreme good and that governments exist primarily to secure human freedom. It is not uncommon in these days to hear " political liberty " referred to almost sneeringly. What good is political liberty, we are asked, to a man out of a job and with a hungry family dependent on him? Is " freedom " an absolute good if it means freedom to starve? Despite the excesses of the totalitarian tyrants, competent observers tell us that there is no term under greater suspicion among intellectuals in Europe today than " democracy." Nor is this tendency confined to Europe; Henry Wallace has warned Americans of the shortcomings of what he calls " Bill of Rights democracy " — which is to say, democracy in the John Locke tradition.

It is perhaps to be expected that the contemporary world anarchy, the sense of encroaching chaos which fills every thoughtful mind with apprehension if not despair, should have made us more anxious to gain security and order than at any time in the last thousand years. Accordingly, the figure of John Locke, which so filled the horizons of political science for our forebears of the eighteenth and nineteenth centuries, today seems to be fading into the shadows. And from a hitherto neglected tomb, from which we of this century have rolled away the stone, we hear the voice of a resurrected

Thomas Hobbes, once more declaring "the mutual relation between protection and obedience," once more calling on men to deliver themselves into the hands of an Almighty State and thereby gain security.

But the result of this swing away from Locke and back toward Hobbes is that we find ourselves again confronted with the figure of Leviathan — the state as "mortal God." And this Leviathan state, because of the added powers which have been placed in its hands by the developing processes of technology, psychology (or, if you prefer, propaganda) and policing comes much closer to usurping the full place and claiming the full authority of a "mortal God" than any state Thomas Hobbes ever knew or conceived. This new totalitarian Leviathan is a jealous "mortal God"; so jealous that it does not hesitate to deny the existence of that "immortal God" whom Hobbes affirmed. Even when it does not join issue with the right to worship the "immortal God," it will not permit men to place obedience to him before obedience to the state. For which reason the relation of religion and the church with the state has taken on, for us who live in this time of Leviathan's return, an importance which too many, including churchmen, have as yet only faintly grasped.

In this book I am trying, in popular terms, to make plain certain aspects of the problem implicit for the churches in the rise of this new Leviathan. But first it is pertinent to ask, Why has this new Leviathan arisen?

II

I shall not here attempt any extended study of the nature and origins of the modern totalitarian state. Already the number of books in English which deal with that subject must have passed well beyond the hundred mark, and there are numerous others in other languages. Some of the best, incidentally, are German and Italian, or at least were written by

Germans and Italians. There is no need, therefore, to go over all that ground again. For our purposes, however, it is necessary to emphasize briefly certain facts in connection with the growth of this new Leviathan, the modern totalitarian state.

We need to remember that totalitarian governments are no new thing in history. Almost any despotism is bound to seek totalitarian controls of the culture within which it exists as well as of the lives over which it rules. And history has never lacked despotisms. Indeed, it is only in comparatively recent times that despotism has ceased to be the most usual form of government. Those who despair because of Europe's swing back toward dictatorships in the third and fourth decades of this century should remind themselves that it is only 156 years since the French Revolution produced its Declaration of the Rights of Man, that it is only 154 years since the American Bill of Rights was written as an amendment into our federal Constitution, and that, as Charles A. Beard has pointed out in *The Republic*, the very word " democracy " has been so suspect that " until well into the nineteenth century, the word was repeatedly used by conservatives to smear opponents of all kinds, whatever the grounds and the differences in opinions." So afraid, as a matter of fact, were even the boldest political leaders of being tarred with the democratic brush that it was not until 1844 that the Jefferson-Jackson party felt it dared to call itself " the American Democracy."

Yet the reminder that totalitarianism is no new thing, in fact if not in name, does nothing to make our contemporary problem simpler. For totalitarianism as we know it seeks a greater measure of control of every aspect of life than most of the despotisms of the past, and because it can command the resources of such modern disciplines as psychology and psychoanalysis it can make this control both pervasive and terrorizing to a degree hitherto unknown. What totalitarianism can do to a rebellious scholar or pastor in a concentration camp is not greatly to be feared; the blood of such martyrs is always the seed of glorious future harvests. But what totalitarianism can do to the complaisant or the compromising scholar or pastor in his *study* — that is to be feared as the doom of civilization.

However, we will never be prepared to deal with the totalitarian threat while we go on so tragically mistaking the causes of its emergence. Listening to men talk about the nature of totalitarianism, one might easily conclude that this affliction has come upon mankind because, all at once, without any discernible reason, a few " bad " men — oh, *very* bad men! — deliberately set out to erect governmental monstrosities. Hence, for many, it seems to follow that when these " bad " men have been defeated, and eliminated, the threat of totalitarianism will have been destroyed, and mankind will return to an evolutionary attainment of perfection in democracy. That, I submit, is hardly an exaggeration of the way in which the herd mind seems to work. Sometimes, to be sure, the blame is laid not so much on " bad " men as on " crazy " ones — fanatics. We must reckon with the rise of totalitarian states, we are told, because Hitler was a megalomaniac or Göring and Hess showed distinct evidences of paranoia, or because the Japanese emperor became a victim of delusions of divinity.

Now, it cannot be denied that the fascist revolutionary movements which gained power in Germany and Italy and in some other countries during the period of the Long Armistice brought to the forefront considerable numbers of unbalanced and abnormal individuals. That is often the case in a revolutionary situation. But this phenomenon of totalitarianism has more behind it than the fanaticism of a few half-cracked adventurers. Hitler and Mussolini did not make totalitarianism; the time was ripe in Germany and Italy, and totalitarianism made Hitler and Mussolini. Do not forget that before there

was totalitarianism in either Italy or Germany, there was the
" monolithic state " in Russia.

It is unfortunate that the bizarre character of the little group
which surrounded Hitler in his rise to power in Germany
should have so distorted the nature of the emergence of modern totalitarianism for a generation of headline readers. Was
Mussolini a fanatic or a maniac? On the contrary, journalists
who knew him longest and observed him most closely have
agreed in reporting that Europe probably contained no more
complete cynic, fully aware of the extravagances of his own
posturings but equally aware of their effect in stampeding
and controlling the Italian people. Was Lenin unbalanced?
Is Stalin? It is doubtful whether modern history can produce
two more cool, detached and balanced minds. Yet between
them, Lenin and Stalin have done far more to make totalitarian
government attractive to millions than any of the fascist dictators have succeeded in doing.

At this point it needs to be observed that many Americans
have been in danger of being beguiled by recent national war
propaganda into attempting to make an impossible distinction
in this matter of fixing attitudes toward totalitarianisms. Because a warring America had certain allies whose feelings must
not be hurt so long as their help was needed to conquer our
national foes, too many of us have tried to rationalize ourselves
into a belief that totalitarianism in itself is not a danger (either
to the church or to the future freedom of mankind), but that
there are good totalitarian states and bad totalitarian states,
and that all we have to oppose is the bad totalitarianism. On
this the position of this book must be made clear at once.

This book is being written under the conviction that all
totalitarian states are a menace, both to the future of the Christian church and to the future freedom of man. It grows out
of the belief that there is inherent in the totalitarian principle

a tyranny, an intolerance, which is the absolute denial of the Christian principle of man's dignity and worth as a son of God. The Christian principle, logically applied, produces the democratic state. The totalitarian principle, logically applied, produces the slave state. A police state is a slave state, no matter what humanitarian ends the police authority may claim to be serving. Wherefore, a totalitarianism based on the dictatorship of the proletariat is just as much a menace to any future based on the Christian view of human destiny as a totalitarianism based on the dictatorship of a fascist élite or of a military oligarchy.

I have felt it necessary to make this position clear lest there be any misunderstanding when it is argued that it is important to see modern totalitarianism, not as the diabolical contrivance of a few perverted men, but as something that has emerged naturally and almost inevitably out of the conditions of modern life. For one thing, we need to realize that this totalitarian drift represents a reaction from the weaknesses, the confusions and especially the irresponsibilities of democratic governments. This, too, is something that has been so often said and so fully documented that it need not be discussed at length. Nevertheless, if, facing the problems left by the war, the democratic states fall back into the suicidal courses that characterized prewar parliaments in much of Europe or into the partisan paralysis too often known in the parliaments of Great Britain and the United States, another totalitarian wave will sweep the world. The Second World War has not vindicated democracy as against totalitarianism — not with Russia coming out of it the principal victor. All the war has done is to postpone the hour of democracy's showdown. But that showdown is implicit in the efforts by which democracy attempts to meet the test of the peace.

However, this negative factor of a reaction against the ineptitudes and irresponsibilities of democracy is not alone

enough to account for the totalitarian resurgence. The emergence of the Leviathan state is also to be seen as still another
product of the industrial revolution. To be sure, it is argued
that the course of the industrial revolution has been toward
a progressive emancipation of mankind from the privations
and ceaseless toil of a peasant and handicraft economy. How
often are we called on, by the celebrants of the power-driven
machine, to rejoice at the improved status of modern man —
with the strength of how-many-hundred horses at his disposal,
with his hours of labor shortened decade by decade, with his
pay (in cash) sufficient to provide him with living conven-
iences and gadgets that a Roman emperor might have envied.
But this contention fails to take into account the trend toward
centralization and concentration that has marked all phases of
the industrial revolution. " Six centralizations," writes Ralph
Borsodi, " characterize modern society: of (1) ownership,
(2) production, (3) population, (4) control, (5) education
and (6) government. These we have rationalized and generally come to accept as (1) monopoly, (2) industrialism,
(3) urbanism, (4) finance capitalism, (5) standardization and
(6) nationalism, under the glowing term of ' progress.' " You
may take such exception as you please to the social philosophy
which Mr. Borsodi derives from this group of facts, but that
these concentrations of power have occurred can hardly be
disputed. Was it not to be expected, then, that the same trend
would extend into the field of government and bring us, not
simply the nationalism which Mr. Borsodi names, but this
super-concentrated form of nationalism which is totalitarianism?

The gravity of our immediate situation arises out of the fact
that as industrialism has developed and concentrated its various forms of power, it has done the same thing with its powers
of destruction. The shudder that went through the world
when it was announced that robot bombs were falling on

London was not caused, at least among the thoughtful, by the accounts of the restricted damage done. But here seemed to be a definite turning point in the history of modern war — the achievement of another level of horror in man's progress toward self-destruction. Here the mechanical ingenuity of man had finally succeeded in inventing a lethal weapon which could be employed over great distances without the use of a human pilot (except at the launching stage), and indiscriminately against soldiers and civilians. Granted that the robot bombs of the recent war were largely experimental affairs which came too late to have any determinative effect on the war's outcome, yet when we remember what happened to the airplane bomber in the twenty brief years between the First and Second World Wars, there is no comfort in the present comparative ineffectiveness of the robots. Industrialism has at last solved the basic problem of making war a contest between machines and men, and the ultimate outcome of this latest technological triumph is likely to be written in blood and agony.

Moreover, there was not an " advanced " country in the war but mobilized its scientists in frantic pursuit of the secret of harnessing atomic energy, in the hope that they might discover a method whereby such destruction could be released as would blow the enemy off the very face of the earth, with all his cities, his factories, his homes, his shrines and his people. It is an edifying exercise to reflect on all these scientists, devoted to the highest ideals of research, many of them often decorated as benefactors of mankind, a good many of them members of Christian churches and professed followers of the Man of Nazareth, shutting themselves in their laboratories and experimenting there night and day, driving themselves ceaselessly, ruthlessly, until they reach the limit of human endurance — for what? All for the hope that they might discover a method of destruction more complete, more impersonal and more beyond any defense than has ever been known before!

If this prospect seems somewhat less than roseate, let me hasten to assure you that such gossip in scientific circles as I hear is confident that American chemists and physicists are far ahead of their scientific rivals in other lands in their pursuit of this devil of atomic energy! *

Technology, in other words, has now reached a point of development where it contains the possibility (some would use a stronger word) of destroying all of us. The same bombing plane which Great Britain, in the disarmament conferences held at Geneva during the Long Armistice, insisted it must have in order to control the tribes on India's northwest frontier, has now come within a narrow margin of blotting out London. Modern wars, and the technological requirements for preparing for them and fighting them, seem to be doing two things. First, they are driving us back to Hobbes's idea of humanity as in a warfare of each against all. And second, they are concentrating power in the great states, while weakening the defenses of all.

The first of these developments results in a general agreement that stability, peace and order are to be obtained only by working out elaborate schemes of policing on a world scale, with such gigantic concentrations of power in the hands of the police that no evildoer will dare lift a finger. To be sure, we do not yet seem to have got around to the solution of that ancient problem, Who will police the police? — but the peace efforts of all our " best " people, who have evidently despaired of any idea of winning peace through a general diffusion of justice, are turned in this direction. The San Francisco Char-

* Early in August 1945, when I began to revise my lecture manuscript for publication, I struck out the last sentence in this paragraph. Then, on August 6, President Truman announced the dropping of the first atomic bomb on Hiroshima, Japan. I have therefore determined, after reflection, to restore the closing sentence exactly as it was delivered at the University of Oregon on February 1, 1945. The only other changes in this paragraph, and in the one preceding, affect the tenses of six verbs. — P.H.

ter sets up a world policing organization of essentially this nature.

The second of these developments is gradually changing the realities of international life until there are only a few nations left with sufficient resources of military potential to render them in any real sense independent or sovereign. Those who cast scorn on the work of Dumbarton Oaks and San Francisco should at least be candid enough to admit that technology has produced a situation in which the small state — unless it lies in such a remote and economically worthless region as Tibet — exists henceforth only on the sufferance of its big neighbors, and that if power and responsibility in international affairs are to be commensurate, we must proceed on a recognition of the enormous power which the machine age has dumped in the laps of not more than three, and quite possibly not more than two, nations. The term Great Powers has been given a meaning by the technology of modern warfare such as it never had before.

III

Is this discussion wandering away from the problem presented by totalitarianism, the new Leviathan? Not at all. We are now, on the contrary, ready to look at the heart of that problem. For the totalitarian declaration is that modern life has become so dangerous that men simply cannot afford the slipshod ways of democracy; that the nation must live, as it were, always under military discipline, always under arms, always on the alert against attack. There have been many definitions of totalitarianism, but one of the simplest and best is that which declares the totalitarian state to be one primarily organized for war and conducted in a perpetual state of war. Even democracies, as we know, tend to go totalitarian in time of war. The states which are totalitarian in time of peace simply deny that peace can be lasting; peace, they hold, is an armistice interval granted to prepare for the next onslaught. It does not much matter whether that onslaught is against them or launched by them against some other state. In either case, they must live continually in the most complete condition of military preparedness which their resources will allow. Their laws remain the laws of a nation at war. Their people are constantly conditioned for conflict. That is the totalitarian state.

Totalitarianism, therefore, is to be considered the effort of nations to face the dangers of the present situation, rather than any diabolical contrivance of wicked men. And so long as those dangers are being multiplied by the terrors born of technology, just so long the sense of insecurity will grow. There are only two ways of attempting to deal with this sense of insecurity. One, which no one as yet is seemingly ready to try except on the most modest scale, is by the Christian method of attempting to do justice and by projecting the principles of the Golden Rule over the whole map of international affairs. Yet even to mention the Golden Rule is to lay oneself open to accusation of being guilty of that most formidable of modern sins — the sin of perfectionism. We may therefore disregard this possibility. The other, which we are all fumbling at, is by repression of the aggressor, either actual or potential. But this, the robot bomb and the atom-smashing laboratory are warning us, means to be ready for attack at any moment. We must expect, as a result, because of the disappearance of all sense of common security among the nations, that long after Hitler has become a name for the historians and mythmakers to quarrel over and Mussolini is remembered only as a rather comic figure with a propensity for balcony scenes, the trend toward a totalitarian regimentation of national life as a measure of safety will continue.

Here, it should be apparent, is a threat to the Christian church of almost incalculable proportions. Consider the extent of the issues raised. This new Leviathan insists that, in order to be ready for any eventuality, the will of the state must control the will of every individual in the state; the Christian church insists that the will of God must prevail over all other wills, whether of men or of their institutions. Leviathan insists that man lives only to perform his duties to the state and that man's life has importance only as a servant of the state; the church insists that every man is a child of God, having infinite worth as an individual and the right to all the freedoms which democracy has proclaimed to be inherent and " sacred " — a term which in itself brings out the religious nature of this present crisis. Leviathan insists that the ultimate fact in the universe is power, and that the morality of the state must therefore be based on its assumption, regimentation and employment of power to overcome all competing powers; the church insists that the ultimate fact in the universe is love, and that all morality, whether of men or nations, must therefore be based on the moral law, which in its essence is the law of love. Leviathan insists that the only security for men and nations is to be found in facing the world in arms, in proceeding on the assumption that all men are potential enemies and that the enemy is never to be granted peace until he has acknowledged the rule of the superior power; the church insists that the only security for men and nations is to be found in doing justice and loving mercy, in proceeding on the assumption that all men are brothers, and that the future order toward which men and nations should strive is to be an order of universal brotherhood.

There can be no lasting accommodation between two such antithetical sets of views and, as recent history should have taught us, there can be no successful compromise. If the conception of the totalitarian state continues to gain ground, the only choice before the Christian church will be that between apostasy and defiance, if need be to the death. We

have every reason to fear that the totalitarian conception will
continue to gain ground. To be sure, some forms of totalitarianism have suffered in prestige from the military outcome
of the recent war — the fascist form exemplified by the European members of the Axis and the military form exemplified
by Japan. But, as has been said, these are by no means the only
forms now competing for men's allegiance.

Moreover, it is the general testimony of those who are most
competent to testify as to what is going on in European
minds that there is no trend more feared in many parts of that
continent than one which might turn toward the disorder, self-
indulgence and irresponsible license which are held to be characteristic of democratic societies. This shying away from
everything that bears the label of democracy is reported to be
especially marked among Continental youth — a particularly
bad sign. We are told that this is a fact to be reckoned with in
every part of Europe except among the youth of the British
Isles and Scandinavia.

Shortly before the end of the European war, the *Saturday
Evening Post* published two unusually revealing articles by
Ernest O. Hauser under the title, "German Prisoners Talk
Your Ears Off" (issues for January 13 and 20, 1945). What
Mr. Hauser wrote was in striking contrast to the superficial
reports of certain correspondents who obviously had neither
the patience nor the mental equipment required to penetrate
beneath the surface defiance shown by young German prisoners. He found these prisoners, while shaken to the core by
the military failure of the Nazis, as skeptical as ever of democracy's capability to cope with the issues of the postwar world.

There is absolutely nothing [wrote Mr. Hauser] a licked German can believe or put his faith in, and the terrific vacuum of his
soul may well be the most important psychological fact in Europe
today. . . . A disillusioned Nazi is a fish out of water, a tree cut
from its roots, a mental case. He is frantic, and acutely unhappy.

He had put everything into Nazism, and it took everything from him. The net result is zero. . . .

Upon superficial investigation these youngsters appear to be true-blue Nazis. They cling to Nazism with the dull despair of the lost souls they are, but, actually, their fangs are rendered harmless with defeat. I have found that, in most cases, they only think they are Nazis. After five or ten minutes, they will admit that the foundation of their faith is shaken or gone, and they will look at you with wide-eyed — and, often, wet-eyed — despair. Can these boys be re-educated?

Mr. Hauser then proceeds to consider some of the possible alternatives to Nazism, as these appeared to young German prisoners just before the final collapse of the Nazi state. Thi is the way he finds the minds of these young men working:

Socialism? Democracy? In 1918, when another beaten German army surged back from France, these words seemed like shiny new toys; they invited an experiment. Today it's different, and all that these Germans can remember is the sad story of the Weimar Republic. I did not find a single German longing for those unhappy days to come back. Confusion goes hand in hand with disillusionment. . . . The only exceptions in this picture of mental bankruptcy are the Communists. The few I talked to knew exactly what they wanted. . . . A disillusioned, defeated, hopelessly perplexed German may find, in the end, that Communism is just the answer to his problems.

When thinking about a report like that, do not forget that a Communist state is a totalitarian state.

The sobering truth is that vast numbers of men, harried and beset as men have been in few previous periods of history, are coming out of these war years believing that their only hope of security lies in the operations of some sort of omnicompetent state. But the omnicompetent state is the totalitarian state; it is Leviathan. The challenge of Leviathan to the church cannot therefore be dismissed or minimized as a passing challenge.   It gives every indication of being, on the contrary, a growing challenge; a challenge that has by no means as yet attained its maximum extent and force.

There is reason to believe, accordingly, that the old issue of church and state, or of church against state, will soon be upon us in a fury unknown for a thousand years.   Are we ready to face that storm?   Do we comprehend from how many quarters it is likely to blow?

CHAPTER II

The Worship of the 'Mortal God'

I

From Constantine to Hitler the pathway of history is marked by the monuments of conflict between church and state. There have been periods when the church has fought to establish its command over the state. There have been periods when the state has struggled to enforce its will upon the church. There have been periods of uneasy neutrality. There have been periods of unholy alliance. " Solutions " have been negotiated (such as the Peace of Augsburg, with its formula — *Cujus regio, ejus religio* — that fastened the faith of the prince on the devotion of the subject) which time has proved abhorrent to men's moral sense. At intervals, communities of the devout, despairing of any accommodation with the pretensions of state authority that would preserve for them the sanctities of their religious beliefs, have sought to withdraw altogether from the society of their fellows. Today, however, the issue between free worship and the power of the state returns in a peculiarly inescapable and aggravated form. This is so largely because the modern state feels itself so insecure. The more it fears itself to be in danger, the more it is driven to demand control of every aspect of the life of its people.

As was said in the previous chapter, the Leviathan which Christians confront today is a " mortal God " in a sense more literal than Thomas Hobbes can be presumed to have had in mind when he coined that designation. To perceive the main outlines of the problems which this new Leviathan creates for religion today, one has but to note that the modern totalitarian state does these three things: first, it presents itself to its citizens as the object of ultimate loyalty; second, it declares that it is the source of ultimate meaning for the individual life; and third, it sets itself up as the custodian of truth. But these are traditionally, and rightfully, the claims and prerogatives of religion. God is the object of our ultimate loyalty. Men's lives find their ultimate meaning in His service. He is truth. The divergence here is complete and fundamental. To employ again the classic phrase of William H. Seward, out of this divergence there arises an " irrepressible conflict."

The result is to be seen in what has actually happened where the Christian church has been required to live and minister under the aegis of avowedly totalitarian states. We still know this story only in part, for the totalitarian state has means of making it very difficult — often virtually impossible — to know what is going on within its borders. But we know that in countries as different as Russia, Germany, Italy and Japan the totalitarian principle has recently produced such tensions with the churches that there have been persecutions, proscriptions and even martyrdoms. Among organized institutions in these nations, frequently it has been only the church which has stood out against the pretensions of absolute state control. It has not done so everywhere or always, but where it has done so it has become a more vital factor in society than at any time for generations past.

At some future time, when more of the evidence is in, it will be possible to discuss at length the experiences of Christian churches and churchmen in dealing with the totalitarian claims of modern states. In the absence of full and dependable information it is possible at present only to refer to certain broad developments as indicative of varied aspects of the problem.

Thus, in Russia, the church faced the opposition of an officially atheistic state, which actively sought its entire suppression, both as a measure of social prophylaxis and control and in recognition of the claims of the alternative Marx-Leninist dogma. That many hundreds of priests were killed, and thousands of churches closed or demolished, during the active phases of this anti-religious crusade, there can be no doubt. That the debased character of much of the priesthood and many of the religious practices in the Russia of the tsars invited such a fate, there can also be no doubt. Recently there has come a change, but who can claim with any confidence that it is a change for the better? Whether Stalin's shift of policy, with its encouragement of a revival for the Russian Orthodox Church, means anything more than a resort to expediency in order to ease Russia's relations with her allies, lessen the fear of Russia in regions invaded by the Red armies and foster a maximum internal unity during the period when the Soviet Union is forced to struggle with the enormous problems of rehabilitation left by the war, we have as yet no way of telling. One suspects not. In any event, there is good reason to place confidence in the reports of those who have talked recently with Stalin and insist that the tales now circulating in church circles which credit him with changed personal views on the worth and legitimacy of religion and the church are sheer myth.

Whatever Russian policy may in time prove to be, one fact which should not be overlooked in the situation as we already know it is that the Orthodox Church has resumed its functioning as a recognized institution in the Soviet Union under conditions which make it almost as wholly an adjunct of the Communist government as it formerly was of the government of the tsars. It is not, to be sure, a department of the government. Stalin is not the head of the Holy Synod, as were the Romanovs (although Stalin, with his theological training, might be better prepared for that role than most of the tsars were). But the revived Russian church functions on terms laid down by the state; it covers the state with adulation and

protestations of unlimited support; it thunders the most terrible anathemas which its vocabulary can compass against all
enemies of the state; the state still owns its houses of worship
and permits their use only at its own pleasure. In other words,
even though the Christian world is still filled with self-con-
gratulation at the recent "favorable turn" taken by church
affairs under Stalin, it has yet to be proved that the church in
Russia is a whit more free, a whit more extricated from the
grip of state totalitarianism, than it was under the tsars. One
difference between the actual status of the church in Russia
today and its status under the Romanovs may prove to be that
the totalitarianism of the Communist state is more efficient in
operation than that of the tsars, so that there may actually
operate a more complete and incessant state check on church
action and thought than Russian Orthodoxy ever knew in its
uninspiring past. A distinguished church leader from the British Isles, recently visiting in this country, reported the apprehension of Anglican churchmen who have watched at first
hand the revival of the Russian Orthodox Church lest this turn
out to be "the most Erastian church in Christian history." *

In Italy, Germany and Japan we have witnessed various attempts to reach a compromise between state claims to totalitarian authority and the church claim to freedom. None has
issued in anything save distress for the church.

Material is almost entirely lacking to study the progress of
this effort by compromise to secure a *modus vivendi* in Japan.
The problem has been made more difficult there by the fact
that the Christian church has represented only a tiny minority
of the population, and that a minority suspected of foreign ties
conducive to national disloyalty. For this reason, Christian
leaders have been under almost unbearable psychological constraint to prove their patriotic devotion — an impulse which

---

* "*Erastian:* one who maintains the theory of the supremacy of the state
in ecclesiastical affairs" (Oxford Dictionary).

the record of churches in the West gives Occidental Christians no right to scorn. From what we now know it would be easy to conclude that the Christian church in Japan during the war all but lost its distinct identity in the synthesis of religious and cultural groups enforced by the state as a means of unifying the Japanese people to meet the national emergency. I expect, however, that when the veil is lifted it will be found that there have been considerable elements in Japanese Christianity which have retained enough independence of the state to provide leadership for a future return to the free principle. It is inconceivable to me that certain Japanese Christians whom I know could ever accept as a permanent basis of church life existence only on terms fixed by the state. At this moment, however, Japan must be regarded as one of the countries where the totalitarian state succeeded in establishing virtually complete control over the church. What the status of the church will be after military occupation is lifted, only time can tell. But unless the post-occupation Japanese state is itself democratized, I can see little prospect for any true freedom for the Japanese church.

The story in Italy has been quite different, and still is clouded in considerable confusion. Not to put too fine a point upon it, the Roman Catholic Church in Italy tried to reach a basis of compromise with the totalitarian state of Mussolini by means of the Lateran treaty of 1929. Offering Mussolini a solution of the troublesome " Roman question " which would help to consolidate his hold on the Italians, the church sought as its share of the bargain acknowledgment of the pope's temporal sovereignty over Vatican City, a recognition of Catholicism's status as the official religion, certain financial considerations, control of education and a privileged missionary position in territories added to Mussolini's revived Roman empire. What it actually got, as the angry protests of the pope made clear, was a most cynical double-crossing from the fascist dictator

— so much so that Pius XI was outraged to the point of writing his encyclical *Non abbiamo bisogno*. In that passionate document, after a direct declaration that the party and regime (the Fascist party, and the Fascist regime, that is) had obtained more from the Lateran treaty than had the church, the pope went on to charge: " Recent events lead us seriously to doubt whether these previous benevolences and favors [from Mussolini] were actuated by sincere love and zeal for religion, or whether they were not rather due to pure calculation and to *an ulterior purpose of domination*." The words which I have italicized point up the issue.

As for Mussolini, once that adventurer had the signature of the papal secretary of state on the dotted line, he did not hesitate to boast to his Chamber of Deputies how completely he had outmaneuvered and rendered impotent the church, reaching his climax in the famous sentence, "We have not resuscitated the temporal power of the popes; we have buried it! " For a fuller treatment of this attempt by a portion of the church to strike a compromise with a totalitarian state, turn to the book by Gaetano Salvemini and George LaPiana, *What to Do with Italy*.* It is true, of course, that when Pius XI and his successor, the present pope, came to realize the one-sidedness of the bargain in which the church had involved itself, they began to try to get free from it. By the time of Mussolini's downfall the pope was one of the most outspoken opponents of the pretensions of state totalitarianism in the Western world. But while Roman Catholics are still trying to rationalize and defend this recent episode in the history of their church, I am confident that with the passage of time it will come to be regarded even in Catholic circles as one of the worst blunders in policy on the record of the modern Vatican.

The crisis through which the church has been passing in Germany is principally of interest not so much because of the

* New York: Duell, Sloan & Pierce, 1943.

heroic resistance offered to Hitler by certain portions of the churches and by certain churchmen — although we record with pride the verdict of Albert Einstein that " only the churches [in Germany] stood squarely across the path of Hitler " — but because what actually occurred there was the failure of a compromise offered by the totalitarian state to the church. In Italy, as has been seen, what took place was the failure of a compromise offered by the church to the state. In Germany it was just the other way round.

Nothing is clearer, as a reading of *Mein Kampf* will show, than that Hitler did not want to become involved in a struggle with the German churches. With the melancholy experience of Bismarck in his *Kulturkampf* before him, Hitler was prepared sufficiently to compromise his principles of totalitarianism to permit the churches, both Roman Catholic and Protestant, to function almost without interference, provided only that they would confine their interests to what was called " the service of the altar." Hitler was quite ready for a concordat with the Vatican (although by no means ready to allow the Vatican to interpret its terms, as the event proved), and in the beginning there seems to have been no suspicion on the part of clergy like Pastor Niemöller that they could not continue their Protestant ministry in full harmony with the Third Reich. Niemöller, it is well to remember, was at first friendly to the Nazi party, socially a conservative, an anti-Socialist and anti-Communist, the pastor of the most fashionable church in Berlin's most fashionable suburb. His congregation was in large measure made up of government officials who had survived from the Hohenzollern days and of Prussian army officers of high rank — which is one reason why it took Hitler so long to put him in a concentration camp. Viewing the church situation as it was in Germany when Hitler came to power, one might have expected that if an offer of compromise from the totalitarian state would work anywhere it would have

worked there. For both Catholics and Protestants were conservative in spirit; both had felt themselves spiritually at odds
with the Weimar republic; neither had done anything to oppose the rise of National Socialism. Moreover, both Catholic
and Protestant tradition was familiar with and favorable to
the idea of a clear-cut delimitation between areas of state and
church control. So when Hitler came offering to respect the
autonomy of the church within the limits of " the service of
the altar," despite the theoretical claims of state totalitarianism, it is not surprising that the first impulse of the churches in
Germany was to accept that offer.

As we know, the compromise did not work. Why not?
The answer is illuminating, especially in the case of the Lutherans. For despite the indoctrination which generations of
German Lutheran pastors had undergone in the necessity of
keeping the church out of entanglement in secular affairs, these
pastors soon found that the actual practice of the totalitarian
state in interfering with church administration (conspicuously
shown, it will be remembered, when the state claimed a determinative voice in the choice of a Reichsbishop), and even more
in controlling the education and activities of youth, left the
minister a prisoner at the altar and threatened the church's very
future existence. The outcome was the revolt of the German
churches against the pretensions of the totalitarian regime —
the only important revolt, as Einstein rightly says, which challenged Hitler until Germany was face to face with military
defeat.

II

But the problem of the totalitarian state is by no means confined to Russia or Japan or Italy or Germany. Not to trace
its menace through all the ostensibly democratic nations, let
us turn to the United States, where I presume we, as patriotic
Americans, would claim that religion is most secure in its

freedom and men in their exercise of freedom of conscience most surely guaranteed against any interference or command by the state. How many Americans realize, or would be willing to admit, that in the United States there has lately been established a complete rule of the state in the realm of conscience, so that it is now the law of the land, as duly interpreted and affirmed by our highest tribunal, that the good citizen must accept the voice of government as the voice of God? Yet that is the case, the verdict of the Supreme Court to that effect having been rendered in 1931 and never reversed. I have in mind, of course, the principle established in the celebrated Macintosh case.

Let me briefly review that case. Douglas Clyde Macintosh, the distinguished professor of theology in the divinity school of Yale University, with a record of honorable service in both the Canadian and American armies in the First World War, applied for American citizenship. He raised no pacifist scruples, but in reply to the question asked all applicants about bearing arms he stated that he was prepared to do so in any war approved by his conscience, but only in such wars. His application for citizenship was rejected. The court of first instance upheld the judgment of the naturalization commissioner; a federal district court of appeals reversed the lower court and ordered Dr. Macintosh naturalized; on appeal to the Supreme Court that body, by the narrow margin of 5-to-4, reversed the reversal, and Dr. Macintosh was debarred. It is true that the margin was only one vote, and it is further true that the dissent was about as distinguished as the Supreme Court, at least in recent times, could muster, consisting, as it did, of Chief Justice Hughes and Justices Holmes, Brandeis and Stone. The dissenting opinion written by Chief Justice Hughes constitutes a memorable document in the history of the struggle for religious freedom. Nevertheless, the verdict of the court went the other way, and that verdict stands to this day, despite all the changes which have since come in the constitution of the court.

Yet that in itself would not be serious were it not for the terms in which the verdict in the Macintosh case was rendered. In denying Dr. Macintosh admission to citizenship the Supreme Court wrote: " When he speaks of putting his allegiance to the will of God above the allegiance to the government, it is evident . . . that he means to make his own interpretation of the will of God the decisive test. . . . We are a nation with the duty to survive; a nation whose Constitution contemplates war as well as peace; whose government must go forward upon the assumption, and safely can proceed upon no other, that unqualified allegiance to the nation and submission and obedience to the laws of the land, as well those made for war as those made for peace, are not inconsistent with the will of God." Note that this does not apply only to the alien seeking naturalization. It is a sweeping and inclusive declaration that our Constitution and laws require that the loyal citizen of the United States must accept any vote of Congress, in time of peace and in time of war, as " not inconsistent with the will of God " — or in other words, as in accord with the will of God! What we are here told is, on the authority of the Supreme Court, that the Constitution under which we live contains an inherent principle by which the right to serve God according to the dictate of personal conscience is limited. Conscience must accept the dictate of the state!

It is true that, as a matter of practical politics, this judgment rendered by the Supreme Court has principally been applied in blocking the naturalization of pacifist aliens. But the *principle*, let me reiterate, as the court lays it down is not confined to aliens. It is declared to apply to all citizens. It was applied by the Supreme Court as recently as 1945 in denying the right of a citizen pacifist to practice in the courts of Illinois. Any

citizen of the United States, to establish his loyalty, must be
ready to accept a vote of Congress as the will of God! No
greater foundation than this is required whereon to erect a
complete structure of state control over men's consciences,
hence over their religious professions, hence over their
churches, hence over the whole position of religion in the
United States. While the Macintosh decision stands, we are
blind fools if we believe that the threat of the " mortal God "
to religious freedom is confined to despotisms overseas.

And lest it be thought that, in thus emphasizing the Macintosh case, I am picking out a single and unparalleled instance
of erratic judicial behavior and giving it an importance which
it does not deserve, reflect upon the fact that within the last
few years, while the tensions were mounting which reached
their culmination in the involvement of the United States in
the war, no cases have given the courts more trouble than
those arising out of the attempt to define (and usually to limit)
the application of the idea of religious liberty to the activities
of that very assertive and cantankerous sect popularly known
as Jehovah's Witnesses. Never before, so far as I know, has
the nation experienced the spectacle of having three members
of the Supreme Court announce that they — not their prede-
cessors — had been wrong in their interpretation of the law in
a previous case, thus inviting the presentation of another case
in which they would have a chance to reverse themselves. Yet
that is precisely what happened in 1942 when, in *Jones* v.
Opelika, Justices Black, Douglas and Murphy appended a
memorandum to their dissent defending the rights of Jehovah's Witnesses to distribute religious literature without a
license, in which they said that a case which they had decided
two years previously (the celebrated Gobitis case in which a
Pennsylvania school board was upheld in requiring a flag sa-
lute from children of Jehovah's Witnesses) had been " wrongly
decided." " Certainly," said this memorandum, " our demo-

cratic form of government, functioning under the historic Bill of Rights, has a high responsibility to accommodate itself to the religious views of minorities, however unpopular and unorthodox these views may be. The First Amendment does not put the right freely to exercise religion in a subordinate position. We fear, however, that the opinions in these and in the Gobitis case do exactly that."

But that is only one of the astonishing developments that have grown out of these Jehovah's Witness cases. A fascinating review of this whole subject may be found in an article in the March 1944 number of the *Minnesota Law Review*, written by Edward F. Waite, retired judge of the district court for the fourth district of Minnesota. Judge Waite lists 31 Jehovah's Witnesses cases that have come before the Supreme Court since 1938 and shows how, on the whole, these have resulted in verdicts which have strengthened or enlarged all civil liberties. " It is plain," says Judge Waite, " that present constitutional guarantees of personal liberty . . . are far broader than they were before the spring of 1938, and that most of this enlargement is to be found in the 31 Jehovah's Witnesses cases. . . . If ' the blood of the martyrs is the seed of the church,' what is the debt of constitutional law to the militant persistency — or perhaps I should say devotion — of this strange group? "

Surely this is a gratifying result from this long succession of cases — a result which one suspects could not have been obtained from the court as it stood at the time of the Macintosh decision. Nevertheless, the closeness of the division in the court in most of these cases, the fact that these cases generally resulted in reversals of lower courts, and the impassioned argument which has accompanied them, in the press as well as in the courts, all should serve to show how far from clear or unreservedly accepted are the rights of churches in the United States to freedom from state repression or control. Or, as

Justice Frankfurter put it in his dissent in one of the most recent Jehovah's Witnesses cases, the West Virginia case: " That which three years ago had seemed to five successive courts to lie within permissible areas of legislation is now outlawed by the deciding shift of opinion of two justices. What reason is there to believe that they or their successors may not have another view a few years hence? . . . Of course, judicial opinions, even as to questions of constitutionality, are not immutable. As has been true in the past, the court will from time to time reverse its position. But I believe that never before has this court changed its views so as to restrict the powers of democratic government. Always heretofore, it has withdrawn narrow views of legislative authority so as to authorize what formerly it had denied. In view of this history it must be plain that what thirteen justices found to be within the constitutional authority of a state, legislators cannot be deemed unreasonable in enacting."

Justice Frankfurter is here arguing, I trust it will be understood, for the right of legislators to enact just such laws for the control of religious bodies as his present brethren on the bench of the Supreme Court by the narrowest of margins have set aside. And he is basing his argument — or appeal, as it might more accurately be designated — on the claim that hitherto the record of the courts has always been to enlarge the controls of government. " Always heretofore," he says, when the Supreme Court has reversed itself and branched out on a new lead, " it has withdrawn narrow views of legislative authority so as to authorize what formerly it had denied." In other words, it may be inferred that it is the view of this distinguished jurist that in the future American legislatures and courts may be expected to impose more rather than fewer state controls over church activities and over the exercise of freedom of conscience.

III

I presume, however, that there are still those who believe that, so far as we here in America are concerned, there can be no real danger to the freedom of religion from state control because the Founding Fathers saw to that when they wrote the guarantee of religious liberty into the first article of the Bill of Rights, and the courts have further strengthened that guarantee by holding that the prohibition against depriving any citizen of his property without due process of law, as contained in the Fourteenth Amendment, applies to his religious freedom. But the guarantee that there shall be no established church and no prohibition of the " free exercise " of religious worship by no means solves the problem of state and church relationships, any more than the guarantees of freedom of speech and assembly, which stand in the same section of the Bill of Rights, have solved the problem which lies behind sedition trials. At the same time the belief, which many seem to hold, that religion has itself provided a solution for this problem in its sacred writings, is equally fallacious.

How often, for example, have we heard appeal made, when this issue of the relations of church and state is under discussion, to the authority of that purported saying by Jesus, " Render unto Caesar the things that are Ceasar's, but unto God the things that are God's." The evidence in favor of the historical accuracy of that statement is very strong. But if it is accepted as a veritable teaching of the Founder of the Christian religion, what does it solve? To begin with, it seems to be a cryptic and evasive aphorism employed by Jesus to turn the edge of a question which presented genuine difficulties. As might be expected, therefore, examination will show that it contains an ambiguity at its vital spot which renders it nearly useless as a rule of action. " Render unto Caesar the things that are Caesar's, but unto God the things that are God's."

All well and good, but the vital question remains: Who determines what is Caesar's and what is God's? Most of the difficulty which the church has encountered in the modern world has arisen out of disagreements over the answer to that question. If the church says, " I determine " (as the Roman Catholic Church, for instance, always does), then the modern state, bursting with nationalistic consciousness and pride, takes violent exception. Witness Mexico! But if the state says, " I determine " (as the modern democratic state, for instance, always does), then the church is likely to find itself called on to agree that the voice of the people is the voice of God, exactly as our Supreme Court asserted in the Macintosh case. No, there is not much help for us in an appeal to this text.

There is even less help, I am sorry to say, in an appeal to that other text sometimes quoted in this connection: " We must obey God rather than men." One reaches this conclusion with regret, for that text has been the rock on which thousands of brave and devoted servants of God have set their feet from the days of Peter and John in Jerusalem right down to Niemöller and Berggrav in the hands of Nazi jailers. Again, however, only a little examination is required to disclose the unresolved dilemma at the heart of this magnificent defiance. " We must obey God rather than men." But who determines when one is listening to the voice of God, and not to the voice of the devil or of the age, or to the echo of one's own voice? Religious history, including that in the Bible, is studded with instances in which devoted men have been sure that they were listening to the voice of God, when their contemporaries — and frequently history — have concluded that what they heard was simply the weird vagaries that float through the mind of the fanatic. America has known a strange conglomeration of religiously fired men and women who were sure that they were obeying God rather than men — the Puritans who hanged Quakers on Boston Common; the Millerites and the Shakers;

Joseph Smith; John Brown of Ossawatomie on the one hand
and the southern divines who upheld the scriptural basis for
slavery on the other; Mary Baker Eddy; William McKinley
in his annexation of the Philippines, to name but a few of
widely differing nature. But the appeal of all these to the im-
mediacy of their spiritual enlightenment has never sufficed to
settle the question whether or not they were authentically inspired of God.

Yet even as we must acknowledge the insufficiency of such
texts in settling the issue of relations between church and state,
we must at the same time recognize that never has the danger
which state totalitarianism constitutes for the church and for
liberty of conscience been more clear. And never have the
reasons for church opposition to all manifestations of the totalitarian spirit been more compelling. For experience by this
time should have taught all churches, whether of the Catholic
or Protestant tradition, that there simply is no ground for
compromise with state totalitarianism. In a totalitarian state
religion must perforce live in bondage, if indeed it lives at all.
The church which tries to compromise with such a state is
simply setting forth on another ride like that of the fabled
young lady of Niger who

>   . . . went for a ride on a tiger,
>   They came back from the ride
>   With the lady inside
>   And a smile on the face of the tiger.

The reason for this basic cleavage between the church and
the totalitarian state lies just where Hobbes put it (though one
may doubt whether Hobbes perceived all the implications of
what he was saying) when he called his Leviathan a " mortal
God." That is to say, it is because this state puts itself in the
place of God by claiming men's ultimate loyalties, by claiming
the right to control conscience, by arrogating to itself judg-

ments of right and wrong, by insisting that the chief end of man is to glorify the state and to exalt it forever — it is because the totalitarian state has become a " mortal God " in this all-embracing sense that the church can never live at peace with it.

Here, in fact, is the point at which the prophetic function of the church is now most required. The church must declare the whole conception of a " mortal God " to be the blasphemy that it is. It must assert the reality of the one, true and only God, who will have no other gods before Him. It must maintain the righteousness and authority of His law. It must warn of His judgments. It must proclaim the autonomy of every soul, the right of every man to freedom of conscience. And if it be objected that freedom of conscience bears within it the danger of human error, then the church should take its stand on the principle never more magnificently expressed than by that contemporary of Hobbes, John Milton, when he wrote in his *Areopagitica:* " Though all the winds of doctrine were let loose to play upon the earth, so Truth be in the field, we do injuriously by licensing and prohibiting to misdoubt her strength. Let her and Falsehood grapple; who ever put Truth to the worse in a free and open encounter? Her confuting is the best and surest suppressing. . . . For who knows not that Truth is strong, next to the Almighty? She needs no policies, nor stratagems, nor licensings to make her victorious; these are the shifts and the defenses that error uses against her power. Give her but room, and do not bind her when she sleeps."

Yet even as we appeal to this great Miltonian principle to vindicate freedom of conscience and of the church from state control, we are compelled to admit that it is a principle utterly rejected by large portions of the church itself. Why should we be surprised, therefore, if the state also rejects it?

CHAPTER III

LEVIATHAN AT WAR

I

When Leviathan goes to war, the issue of the relationship between church and state becomes most acute. For, as has already been said, a modern state making war must of necessity go totalitarian. It may not go totally totalitarian (if such a "bull" may be permitted), but the longer the war lasts, the more danger of defeat grows, the more inevitably will it take on complete totalitarian controls. It makes no difference how devoted its people may be to democracy as a principle; when every resource of the nation must be thrown into a battle for survival, nothing less than totalitarian controls will suffice.

Both Great Britain and the United States have learned this again in the recent conflict. Habeas corpus meant nothing to the eighteen hundred Englishmen who were imprisoned without arraignment or trial until Britain had disposed of Hitler. And had not Hitler fallen when he did, the United States would eventually have put into force the National Service Act demanded by the President which would have given the government power to tell every citizen of working age where he must work, under what conditions, at what pay and for what hours. As it was, the war subjected Americans to more extensive and severe controls, affecting all aspects of life, than would have been dreamed possible a few years ago. Even the churches learned that they could hold denominational meetings only at such times and places, with such attendance and for such purposes as the government approved.

One may view this development with apprehension, but

not with surprise. The military men are right in their contention that modern wars cannot be waged on any other basis. Modern wars are " total " wars, and total wars require totalitarian controls. Total wars are fought by total populations. The so-called civilian population which produces the munitions to keep the armies in action is as essential a part of the war machine as the troops in uniform. That is why the airplane bombing of factory districts, rail centers and communication lines hundreds of miles from the fighting fronts, horrible as is its destruction of civilian life and homes, can still be defended by the military authorities as a logical and even necessary development of modern warfare. The German planes that blasted Coventry, the British planes that blasted Hamburg, the American plane that wiped Hiroshima off the map were simply trying to do the same thing that Sherman did on his march through Georgia eighty years ago — render a region incapable of supporting the armies in the field. It is the *nation* that makes modern war, and the technique of winning victory is dependent even more on overcoming the nation's will to fight by undermining its morale than on winning strategic battles. The matter of public morale therefore becomes of supreme importance to the war-making state, and it is in that realm, of course, that the church is held to have a definite and major responsibility.

For the Christian church, this problem of its relationship to the necessarily totalitarian war-making state has attained a new tension because the church is plagued by the moral problem of war as it never has been before. It may perhaps be going too far to say that large portions of the church have lost, or are losing, faith in the possibility of a just war. But I do not think it an exaggeration of the situation to say that there are millions of Christian churchmen who, while they may still argue the theoretical possibility of a just war and the inevitable implication of the citizen in any modern war fought by a state of which he is a part, nevertheless are to this extent ready to adopt the pacifist position — that they no longer have any confidence that wars achieve the ends for which they are proclaimed. They regard with sorrow and with some consternation, but without much surprise, the progressive whittling down of the high moral and political purposes customarily avowed when fighting starts. They are resigned to seeing these gigantic struggles of peoples degenerate into bloody battles for survival, which leave the same issues that are alleged to have caused the war confronting mankind at the end, and often in more difficult and trouble-breeding forms.

What prospect, for example, is there that the recent war, when its results are finally clear, will be found to have solved or removed the problem of economic inequality between " have " and " have-not " peoples, or the problem of human freedom which is all bound up in imperialism? Has Poland been left less exposed to invasion by an outside tryanny, has her independence been secured beyond what it was before Great Britain and France intervened to stop Hitler's aggression? Or is the " solution " of the Polish question which the war has brought any more likely to preserve the peace of Europe than were the Polish decisions of the Treaty of Versailles? If the war in the Pacific fundamentally grew out of a determination to safeguard the territorial integrity and national sovereignty of China, does the outcome point to the achievement of that end? And if the Second World War, considered as a global whole, is said to have been caused by fear lest a military tyranny bestride Europe and reach toward world power, has its result done away with the burden of militarism or left any nation where it feels more secure unless it is armed to the teeth? Is the outcome of the war producing the ends for which President Roosevelt and Mr. Churchill said they were fighting, or were ready to fight, when they drew up the Atlantic Charter? Is it producing a just and lasting peace?

The result of facing questions such as these is that great numbers of Christian churchmen, although they "supported the war effort," did so with such divided minds and faltering enthusiasm that they were frequently said to fight "sorrowfully," and without illusion. Arthur Koestler, that significant product of a European radicalism which has lost faith in Russian communism, in the closing stages of the war said of his fellows: "We all more or less feel that we fight this war rather *in spite of* than *because of* something. The big words and slogans rather embarrass us, we don't like to be thought quite so naïve as that." * Koestler's words might be applied without straining to the war participation of many a churchman.

There was, moreover, a widespread demand that the churches should bear their part in the national war effort "repentantly," and church resolutions called forth by the war were peppered with that term. To fight repentantly, in most cases, meant no more than to fight sorrowfully, to fight regretfully, to fight remorsefully. This, it hardly needs to be pointed out, is to prostitute a great word in the vocabulary of religion. There can be no true repentance without a faithful effort to turn away from the sin of the past and to commit it no more. So far, there is little evidence on the part of individuals, and none at all on the part of states, of determination to abjure the sins of competitive nationalism and imperialism which brought on this tragedy. It is a perversion of the truth to say that Christians in any significant numbers fought the Second World War repentantly. But it is true that Christians in very great numbers fought it reluctantly, skeptically, and with a sense of moral revulsion. The Second

* *The Yogi and the Commissar.* New York: Harcourt, Brace & Co., 1945.

World War proved to be a war of galley slaves — slaves of the totalitarian state!

II

If space permitted, it would be rewarding to trace the changes that have marked church thinking and action on the subject of war in recent years. There are, however, so many studies of the subject that we need not go into it at any length here. The amount of effort which Christian thinking, from Augustine on, has devoted to the attempt to define the nature of a just war sufficiently testifies to the problem which war has historically created for the Christian conscience. Nevertheless, there can be no mistaking the new intensification of this problem which has come with the total wars of the present era. And now the atomic bomb creates an almost intolerable burden for the Christian conscience.

The change in the attitude of the churches to the war-making state is well illustrated for American churches by the contrast between the reaction of the churches to our war with Spain in 1898 and their reaction to the recent conflict. There have been few wars which, in retrospect, have appeared more senseless, more cynical or more inspired by dubious motives than the war of 1898. Walter Millis, in his study of that war, *The Martial Spirit*,* treats it as a gigantic *opéra bouffe*. But it was more than that. As Senator Hoar of Massachusetts accurately told the United States Senate at the time, it was a war to wrench the nation out of its whole tradition and to involve it in all the perversions of democracy implicit in a plunge into imperialistic aggrandizement. Looked back on from today's vantage point, it is hardly too sweeping a judgment to say that every moral pretension under which the war was fought from 1898 to 1901, when resistance finally ceased in the Philippines, is now under suspicion if not outrightly condemned.

* Boston: Houghton Mifflin Co., 1931.

Yet — and here is the fact to notice — it may be doubted whether any war in modern times has received more complete, enthusiastic and sustained support from the Christian churches. To them it was, almost without exception, a Christian crusade, which reached its grand culmination and final religious justification at that unforgettable scene in the White House when President McKinley said to the delegation of Methodist bishops who had called to assure him of God's approval for the annexation of the Philippines:

The truth is I didn't want the Philippines, and when they came to us as a gift from the gods, I did not know what to do with them. . . . I sought counsel from all sides — Democrats as well as Republicans — but got little help. . . . I walked the floor of the White House night after night until midnight; and I am not ashamed to tell you, gentlemen, that I went down on my knees and prayed Almighty God for light and guidance more than one night.

And one night late it came to me this way — I don't know how it was, but it came: (1) That we could not give them back to Spain — that would be cowardly and dishonorable; (2) that we could not turn them over to France or Germany — our commercial rivals in the Orient — that would be bad business and discreditable; (3) that we could not leave them to themselves — they were unfit for self-government — and they would soon have anarchy and misrule over there worse than Spain's was; and (4) that there was nothing left for us to do but to take them all, and to educate the Filipinos, and uplift and civilize and Christianize them, and by God's grace do the very best we could by them, as our fellow men for whom Christ also died. And then I went to bed and went to sleep and slept soundly.

It is sometimes said that the Spanish-American war drew its inspiration largely from the craze for circulation of the Pulitzer and Hearst newspapers, both new phenomena at that time in American journalism, both utterly without scruple in their methods of appealing to the mass appetite for sensation. A study of the church papers of that period, however, will show that they glorified that sordid conflict as a Christian crusade for righteousness and freedom fully as uncritically as did the daily press.

All this is worth recalling as a measure of the change in church thinking that has taken place in less than fifty years. Few Christian churchmen today can read President McKinley's speech to the bishops without a queasy feeling. Churchmanship of the McKinley type now looks like a species of indecent mental exposure; we find it hard to believe that so recently a devout American churchman could think and talk in that way without cant, or American bishops receive such a statement as evidence of the indubitable workings of Divine Providence. For we stand with all the searching of mind that went on among the churches during the Long Armistice between us and that day.

Not all the conclusions of that armistice period seem as valid today for many of us as they did at the time. For instance, even the ministers who maintained their personal pacifism during the recent war are likely to feel that there was too much oversimplification, too much swimming with the tide in the results of the famous *World Tomorrow* poll in 1926. In that poll (participated in by 20,870 clergymen, an astonishingly high percentage of the entire Protestant ministry in the United States, as anyone who has tried to get answers to a questionnaire can testify) 42 per cent said that they were unwilling to serve even in a defensive war; 66 per cent said that the Christian church should refuse to sanction or support *any* future war; and 77 per cent favored disarmament by the United States regardless of the action of other countries. At the same time Canon " Dick " Sheppard, the impatient parson, was founding his Peace Pledge Union in England, in which hundreds of British clergy vowed that they would never again participate in or support a war. I do not recall such episodes for any purposes of criticism. What was then going on among the clergy of England and America was only a reflection of the public disillusionment with the outcome of the First World War. While English parsons joined " Dick " Sheppard in the Peace Pledge Union, you will remember, the sons of the British aristocracy, meeting in the Oxford Union, upheld by majority vote a resolution " that this house will in no event fight for king and country." And pacifist societies flourished on practically every American college campus.

But the revulsion of the churches against war in its modern form went beyond personal pacifism. It went into an examination of the moral pretensions of war as an institution, and a widespread rejection of its claims. It was not only American church bodies which during the Long Armistice adopted resolutions holding that war is by its nature a denial of the gospel of Jesus Christ and therefore to be opposed by the church (dozens of resolutions to that effect could be quoted), but when the representatives of ecumenical Christianity gathered in that most famous of modern church councils at Oxford in 1937, they registered their deliberate judgment that since " war involves compulsory enmity, diabolical outrage against personality, and a wanton distortion of the truth," it is " a defiance of the righteousness of God as revealed in Jesus Christ and Him crucified."

In other words, it seems well within the truth to say that the end of the Long Armistice found the Christian church, at least in the Occident, thoroughly disillusioned as to the nature of modern war, the gains to be expected from it, or its effect upon the morality of men and nations. Whatever might happen under the pressures of a state at war, allegedly fighting for its existence, the effect of these conclusions, reached over that twenty-year period, could not be wholly eliminated.

III

Then came the war. The churches, which had so widely proclaimed their loss of confidence in the moral pretensions of war, found themselves living in communities that were at war. In every case these communities were told that they were fighting in self-defense; in every case the majority mind accepted that justification for fighting; in every case the government, in order to procure the necessary maximum war effort, moved toward totalitarian controls. How would the churches act in such a situation? I present this account only as a personal and tentative report, for I am well aware that fuller information, which will not be available until the full history of the war is written, may render necessary revisions in some of my conclusions, and I also know that my personal views are certain to have affected my judgment in some particulars. But this, I should say, speaking in generalizations, is about what happened:

As the governments went to war they expected the same unquestioning support from the churches they had been able to count on in the past. It must have come as a distinct shock, therefore, to the authorities in Great Britain, Canada and the United States to find that they could command from the churches no such instant and all-out endorsement as the national emergency seemed to demand. There were, to be sure, professions of loyalty. For instance, the Roman Catholic hierarchy in this country — the weight of whose influence had, on the whole, been against America's entrance into the war — adopted a resolution which practically endorsed the government's war policies and efforts. But this resolution stood out almost alone among those of the major communions in its flag-waving propensities. Most of the Protestant churches backed and filled, blew hot and cold, struggled to achieve forms of words in their resolutions that would satisfy the patriotism of their members without committing themselves to the proclamation of a holy war — on the whole a confused and sometimes confusing performance which at last left the government without any religious sanction of being engaged in a sacred crusade, and frequently, I think it fair to say, left many of the members of the churches in doubt as to the degree of approval with which their churches regarded their individual participation as fighters.

As an illustration of the confused course which this effort by the state to command the all-out blessing of the church followed, consider what happened in meetings of the Northern Baptist Convention after Pearl Harbor. I choose this denomination for illustrative purposes because it is so democratic in organization that it cannot be suspect of being controlled by any inner hierarchy, and the " messengers " to its annual conventions represent a characteristic cross section of middle class American Protestanism. In May 1942 the Northern Baptists, meeting at Cleveland five months after Pearl Harbor, had before them a resolution, introduced by the president of their previous convention, which said:

In this day of decision we reaffirm our allegiance to the government and people of the United States in the war in which thousands of our sons and brothers are engaged for the preservation and assured maintenance of those essential freedoms won by generations of heroic men and women.

In the tense debate, it was freely alleged that this resolution had been introduced on direct prompting from the White House, and some of its supporters relied on that allegation as a source of strength. By the close vote of 369 to 337 it was, however, defeated. Instead, the convention adopted this:

We affirm our position on war taken through the years in the resolutions of this convention and repent of our sin in not making Christ's way more effective. . . . We express our willingness to do anything for the welfare of our country, regardless of personal cost or sacrifice, which lies within the full sanction of our individual consciences.

That is to say, the Baptists made exactly the same reservation concerning the superior rights of conscience which the Baptist theologian, Professor Macintosh, was denied citizenship for making.

Because of war conditions, there was no Northern Baptist Convention in 1943. In 1944, however, the denomination met again, this time at Atlantic City. In a dramatic scene one of the denomination's best known ministers, who had lost a son in the war and announced that he sought suspension of the rules and immediate recognition because he was to depart on a secret mission for the government within an hour, secured an unexpected access to the platform long enough to obtain adoption, by a heavy majority, of a resolution which contained such passages as these:

The church must be the church, not a recruiting agency for any government. She must build morale and strengthen the foundations. . . . Wherever the battle joins with evil . . . " fair as the morning " she must be " as militant as an army with banners." . . . War itself is not and cannot be made holy. . . . But while war itself is unholy, liberty and justice, brotherhood and human personality are most holy. For the overwhelming majority of all those who seek to know the mind of Christ . . . when war is invoked against these holy things there is no alternative but to dedicate in their defense our lives, our treasure and . . . the lives of our children. . . . *We do not pray for man's mere triumph over his brother man, for " all have sinned and come short " and each is to God equally precious, but " God has a stake in this war " and we dare not wait to achieve perfection before we rise to defend freedom and to battle for a righteous cause.* . . . We will not bless war but we will not withhold our blessing from our sons who fight and from our country's cause.

On the next day, however, the convention, evidently believing that it had been stampeded into an action which did not represent its real convictions, reconsidered this resolution, deleted the phrase about the church being " as militant as an army with banners," substituting " as a messenger of Christ," and finally struck out the entire sentence which I have italicized. To complete its action, the convention then approved the recommendation of its resolutions committee that the resolutions of previous conventions on war (including the one adopted in 1942, quoted previously) be reaffirmed.

There the Northern Baptists stood until the end of the war. One can hardly blame individual Baptists if they found this record somewhat confusing. It does reveal, however, that this denomination was not swept into uncritical support of the national war program. Similar reports could be brought from other denominations.

IV

If one were to generalize, it would not miss the mark by much to say that in the recent war most of the churches tried to do three things: (1) to hold back the armies from methods of waging war which outrage all humanitarian sentiments and to warn the belligerent peoples against such hate, self-righteousness and demand for revenge as would make more difficult reconciliation after the conflict; (2) to protect the rights of conscience of such church members of draft age as felt compelled to refuse to perform any military service; (3) to propose war aims and peace terms that would make possible a " just and durable " peace. In addition, the churches of course carried on their usual ministries to those in the armed services, and gave invaluable aid to such causes as the Red Cross, the relief of devastated countries, and the U.S.O. But there was little use of church facilities to help in the sale of war bonds, and recruiting sermons were all but unknown. The positive contribution of the churches to the war effort followed the three lines of activity which I have enumerated.

In the light of the record, it must be acknowledged that the churches by no means accomplished these purposes. They were not, in the first place, able to keep the methods of waging war within limits of humanitarian concern that would respect their opposition to brutality. On the contrary, they found that war is inherently brutal, and that modern war inflicts its brutality indiscriminately. One of the most sobering illustrations of this concerned the so-called " obliteration bombing " to which both American and British airforces resorted. Several times during the war groups of respected Christian leaders in England and the United States issued agonized protests against the bombing policies followed by the airforces of their countries. The daily press generally belittled these as " pacifist " aberrations, but the Christian conscience was left disturbed. After the atomic bombs fell on Japan, this distress reached such proportions that, had the war lasted much longer, serious tension might have developed between the churches and the American government. As events transpired, however, only individual churchmen and unofficial church publications wrestled with the moral problems created by the modern bomber.

Especially moving were the valiant efforts which that great Christian publicist, Dr. J. H. Oldham, made in his *Christian News-Letter* of London to work out principles of bombing which could gain the assent of the Christian mind. Probably no Christian publication in the world worked harder than Dr. Oldham's *News-Letter* to discover a Christian apologetic for the war or a justification of the deeds of Christians taking part in it. The more meaningful, therefore, was its failure to formulate any " Christian " rules of bombing that could appear other than laughable to young men required to release their bombs while five or six miles above the earth, often with heavy blankets of clouds blotting out the targets, or at night, and usually while trying to dodge anti-aircraft fire. The impossibility of controlling the destruction spread by such operations was shown by the fact that in both the Italian and German campaigns there were tragic instances in which we bombed our own soldiers and our own positions. We even killed one of our own top-ranking generals in this fashion. In the face of the brutal facts, accordingly, Dr. Oldham was at last forced to fall back on the position that the Christian conscience can approve no bombing which is not certified by the military authorities as falling within the category of " military necessity." Yet even he, I am sure, must have been aware, in the depths of his mind, that such a limitation is no limitation at all. There are few horrors which have not been justified by warriors as " military necessity." I have no doubt some German generals believe that unutterable atrocities such as Lidice and the death chambers in which Jews were exterminated in Poland were military necessities. And few American generals would hesitate for an instant to certify that the use of atomic bombs was also a military necessity even though Hiroshima and Nagasaki were wiped out after Japan's navy had been sunk, her airforce destroyed, her homeland blockaded, her supplies cut off and the military decision already rendered beyond all possibility of doubt!

Again, the churches cannot extract much satisfaction from the results of their efforts to protect the rights of conscience of objectors to war service. In this respect, the churches of the United States were not able to do as much as those in England. This is an involved subject to which we cannot afford to give the attention it deserves. Any who may be interested in pursuing it should read *The Conscientious Objector and the Law* and *Conscience and the State* * by Julien Cornell, the New York lawyer who served as counsel to the committee

* New York: John Day Co., 1943, 1944.

on conscientious objectors of the American Civil Liberties Union. But as a measure of the church's failure to obtain its desired ends in this matter, consider the fact that there were more than seven times as many c.o.'s in prison in the United States in this as in the last war; that more than half the population of the great federal prison at Danbury, Connecticut, was made up of c.o.'s; that a sixth of the entire federal prison population of the nation was made up of c.o.'s; that prison sentences passed on these martyrs to conscience averaged 30.6 months, although the average sentence for all federal prisoners is only 22.1 months (sentences for conscientious objection in fact averaging longer than for violations of the narcotics laws, the liquor laws, the white slave laws and the postal laws); that there were fifteen times as many c.o.'s in prison in this country as in Great Britain, although there were more objectors in Great Britain; and that among the c.o.'s not in prison but in the Civilian Public Service camps there was endless debate and at times almost open revolt because of a widespread belief that the means approved by the churches to safeguard the rights of conscience actually operated so as to obscure and even compromise the " testimony " which the c.o.'s were trying to offer.

And finally, the churches can hardly derive much satisfaction from the results of their efforts to induce the victors to write a " just and durable peace." To be sure, there is reason to believe that church study and discussion of the problems of postwar organization and the positions announced at such a church conference as was held at Cleveland in January 1945, had something to do with the improvements made in the Dumbarton Oaks proposals at the San Francisco conference of the United Nations. Church agitation also undoubtedly contributed to the speedy and almost unanimous ratification of the United Nations Charter by the United States Senate. But the San Francisco conference did not write the peace. The peace, as the terms which come from the closely guarded meetings of the Big Three show, is turning out to be cruel, ruthless, vindictive and hate-breeding.

The peace following this war is wrong in the same way that the peace of Versailles was wrong, and its detailed provisions are proving to be even more brutal than the provisions of Versailles. The peace is making a mockery of the Atlantic Charter. It is slamming the door of hope not only in the faces of millions of our erstwhile enemies, but equally in the faces of millions of our friends and allies in small nations and in dependent areas who once looked to the prospect of Allied triumph as the harbinger of their security and freedom. The only basis on which this peace can hope for even a limited endurance is that Russia and the United States, because they have the military power, will ram it down the throats of the rest of the world's peoples, and keep it rammed down — and will not fall afoul of each other in so doing. But what resemblance has any such prospect as that to the peace of justice and mutuality and hence durability that the churches declared they were seeking?

V

Something should be said, before leaving this phase of the subject, about the part played by the pope during the war. On the whole, I believe that Pius XII must be credited with having played a worthy and humane role. He, too, sought to induce all the belligerents to forego methods of warfare repugnant to humanitarian instincts. He, too, warned against the growth of hate or of a demand for vengeance. And he, too, tried to implant in the minds of governments the principles of a just peace. As early as his Christmas allocution of 1939 the pope laid down his basic five peace points: (1) that the security and independence of *all* nations must be safeguarded; (2) that there must be general disarmament; (3) that there must be an international organization to insure the loyal execution of all international agreements; (4) that the economic needs of all nations and peoples must be fairly met; and (5) that the peace settlement must be in accord with the moral law. Following that initial pronouncement, with each succeeding Christmas allocution Pius XII made more specific his peace proposals. In his 1944 allocution he warned the victors that if the peace is to be more than another Long Armistice they must recognize in it the unity of nations by providing for quick entrance into the general postwar organization by enemy as well as neutral states.

Unfortunately, the effect of the pope's efforts to secure a generous and lasting peace was seriously weakened by the devious course pursued by Catholic leaders in protecting what they conceive to be the political interests of the Vatican. The Vatican claims to take a neutral position as regards all forms of government which permit the church to function freely. But in the actual situation which is emerging in Europe, so at a loss for a program are most " liberal " elements and so ready is communism to push forward its program as a means of keeping the Continent free from reactionary controls, that the Vatican is finding itself in the same difficulty which beset Mr. Churchill during the waning months of his prime ministership. That is to say, when the Vatican now shows preference for non-Communist or anti-Communist regimes, it is in danger of becoming popularly identified as a champion of extreme conservatism if not black reaction.

It is instructive to follow the series of addresses and state papers in which Pius XII has been struggling to free the Roman Church from that accusation. They have been extremely able arguments. But he is almost hopelessly handicapped by the record. European democrats have not forgotten that, in February 1929, the pope's predecessor, Pius XI, called Mussolini " a gift of Providence, a man free from the prejudices of the politicians of the liberal school." They do not forget that 57 bishops and 19 archbishops in Italy, on the day the League of Nations met to consider the assault on Ethiopia, sent a joint telegram to the Fascist dictator: " Catholic Italy thanks Jesus Christ for the renewed greatness of the country made stronger by Mussolini's policy." They recall that message of congratulation which Pius XII himself sent to Franco at the victory of reaction over the republican forces in Spain: " With great joy we address you, dearest sons of Catholic Spain, to express our paternal congratulation for the gift of peace and victory, with which God has chosen to crown the Christian heroism of your faith and charity, proved in so much and so generous suffering." And when the pope now tries to persuade the world which is emerging from the war that Catholicism has never favored fascism over other forms of government, he must struggle against the recollection of such sayings as that of Cardinal Gasparri, the former papal secretary of state: " The Fascist government of Italy is the only exception to the political anarchy of governments, parliaments and schools the world over," and of Cardinal Hinsley of London: " If Fascism goes under, nothing can save the country from chaos. God's cause goes with it." *

In the light of such a record, what chance has the papacy of persuading Europe's survivors that Roman Catholicism may be depended on to resist the rise of reaction or to defend human liberty and the freedom of democratic societies?

VI

But all that the churches, Protestant and Roman Catholic, had been able to do to mitigate the horrors of the recent war was reduced to futile frittering in one lightning blast which

---

* All the quotations in this paragraph are taken from *Vatican Policy in the Second World War*, by L. H. Lehmann. New York: Agora Publishing Co., 1945.

shook the world in the closing days of the conflict. The atomic bombs which blasted Hiroshima and Nagasaki ushered in a new day for mankind — a day which may see loosed powers of destruction so terrible that man himself may not survive. It is, of course, true that the release of atomic energy carries with it potentialities for good as well as for evil. Yet the scientists who produced the atomic bomb agree that it will be decades before this blinding energy will be harnessed for constructive purposes. And it is not without significance that this discovery is the first of man's basic triumphs which has been gained in a search for methods of destruction. All the other fundamental discoveries and inventions of man's past — fire, the wheel, the lever, the boat, the compass, numbers, the internal combustion engine — have first been attained to enrich and enlarge human existence. Even gunpowder was first used, when invented by the Chinese, to heighten festival celebrations. With the atomic bomb, man has penetrated one of the final secrets of nature for the primary purpose of destroying his fellow man.

It is no wonder that the explosion of the first atomic bombs threw almost as great a fright into the peoples of the conquering nations as into the people of Japan. Despite all official reassurances as to the closeness with which the secret would be guarded by the United States, Great Britain and Canada, all thoughtful men realized that it would soon become the property of most of the nations. Sir James Chadwick, who headed the group of British scientists which helped to produce the bomb, was simply confirming the reasoning of the common man when he said that any nation, given the necessary raw materials, could work out the principles of the atomic bomb within five years without recourse to the American-British-Canadian formulas. Few doubted that the German scientists who had been credited with being so near success in this race for death, would find as warm a welcome in Moscow as did the officers of the German general staff after the First World War.

In other words, mankind must now accept that within the next five years most large nations will be able secretly to manufacture a sufficient number of these pulverizing weapons of destruction so that, if they are discharged from high-speed stratospheric airplanes or from the ocean-spanning robots which were on the drawing boards when the war ended, they will be capable of wiping out the centers of resistance of an enemy in the first half-hour of a surprise war. No H. G. Wells ever conceived such a nightmare future for humanity. Yet this is no stuff of which bad dreams are made; this is the fate which has now in actuality come upon us.

For the churches, however, the advent of the atomic bomb brings a crisis even more inescapable than that which now confronts the political and educational institutions of our society. What moral controls can hold this monster in check? What moral virtues can persist in its presence? Talk about humane methods of waging warfare, about the rights of conscience, about a peace which establishes universal freedom from fear, becomes infant prattle when confronted by the reality of this illimitable power. The United States destroyed any hope that traditional moral controls could be established when it unleashed the atomic bomb against an enemy already defeated without offering to that enemy any of the easily accessible methods by which to determine the existence and destructive nature of this new weapon.

The very moral pretensions with which the United States was fighting now create for the churches the inescapable question: Can they admit that *any* state is fit to act as the custodian of such potential destruction? If Lord Acton's word as to the absolute corruption worked by absolute power is true, does this not argue that the entire concept of separate sovereignties, each in possession of this power of life or death over its fellows, is one on which the blessing of the moral law and of the church can no longer rest? To save humanity, must not the churches now demand an end to the sovereign nation-state?

In certain quarters there is rejoicing because the atomic bomb has rendered obsolete the concept of mass armies, based on universal conscription, against which many of the churches in the West have protested. Even the vested interests of a professional fighting class and of a munitions industry will not long be able to keep the conscript system alive after it is generally realized that wars have now become a matter of the labor of a comparatively small number of highly trained experimental scientists and technicians, and of possessing an armory of these lethal weapons. But the end of conscription is a matter of such comparatively minor consequence that the churches can never regard it as compensation for the awful problems which this new terror has brought in its train.

There must be, for example, realization that with the invention of the atomic bomb the power of tyrants and of the tyrant-state is multiplied out of all recognition. What reality, one may well ask, remains in the " democratic " conception of war as something undertaken only by the will of the people expressed through a vote of Congress? When the successful employment of atomic power in warfare depends upon resort to it secretly, suddenly, in the first thirty seconds of an unannounced conflict — and this, it must be repeated, will be the case, according to the highest authority, any time after the next five years — a nation that allowed itself to be hampered by such " democratic " restrictions as are embodied in the Constitution of the United States would simply be courting national destruction. The atomic bomb, in the present divided state of mankind, is an invitation to all future Hitlers.

In sober truth, with this development the problem of war has become insoluble in national terms. Moral distinctions between " right " nations and " wrong " nations have ceased to have meaning. Any effort to define a " just " war is as futile as would be an effort to define a " just " earthquake. From now on, if the pattern of jealous and separate sovereignties persists, nations will be divided only between the atomically armed and the unarmed — those that are in a position to back their will by the ruthless use of this awful weapon and those that are unable to employ or counter it. Between nations thus armed, any pause to give warning before striking will be fatal, for in that moment while the blow is withheld the enemy will have his chance to strike to the death.

Hence it appears that from now on the only countervailing method that will suffice to save mankind is a new world order. It must be an order in which a genuine world authority will supersede the sovereignty of nations, in which national armies, national arsenals, national policies will be a thing of the past. In this atomic age, if the Christian church seeks peace it must seek a world government. For when faced by the threat of atomic destruction, all national sovereignties will be driven irresistibly into the form of the Leviathan state. Yet they will take that form only to perish.

VII

Out of all this sense of tension between the churches and the great war-making states of the contemporary period there has naturally arisen, on the part of thoughtful Christians, a call for more thorough and deep-going studies of the issues involved. The result has been a series of significant pronouncements on the relation of Christians, and of the Christian church as an institution, to the war, and to war as an institution. One of the most thoughtful of these has come from the Baptists of the Maritime Provinces of Canada. Another is being issued in parts — it is not yet completed — by a special commission of the Church of Scotland under the chairmanship of Professor John Baillie. There have been others; an examination of them all is beyond the possible scope of this book. For our purposes, however, the most important of these documents is that published in November 1944 by the commission of twenty-six American theologians, headed by Professor Robert L. Calhoun of Yale, which was commissioned by the Federal Council of Churches to draw up a report on " The Relation of the Church to the War in the Light of the Christian Faith." The result is a 25,000-word document which has been called " the noblest and most illuminating statement of the Christian faith, of the nature of the church, of the relation of the church to the war, of the numerous problems which the war presents to Christian faith . . . and of the crisis through which contemporary civilization is passing, which has ever been produced by American Christian scholarship." Since I can do no more than briefly summarize a few of the most important conclusions stated in this report, any who may have more than a superficial interest in the effort of the churches to escape from the clutches of the war-making Leviathan should get this document and carefully study its entire text.

To begin with, what does this report of the Calhoun commission have to say about the nature of the state, and the relation of the church to it?

The state as the chief earthly custodian of law is regarded by most Christians as in principle a pattern of life divinely ordained to safeguard social order against anarchy, justice against injustice. On these grounds it has a just claim to the loyal support of Christian citizens in the performance of its proper duties. It has no just claim to absolute or unconditional authority even within its own territorial bounds. In relation both to its own subjects and to other states or persons, it is bound by the demands of that divine order often denoted by the terms natural and moral law, that is binding upon all men and human institutions. The modern secular theory of ultimate sovereignty for each existing state cannot be justified to Christian faith.

The reservations in such a passage as this are even more important than the affirmations. The state has a just claim on the loyalty of Christians as long as it confines itself to its " proper duties." It has no " unconditional authority." It is bound by the " moral law." It has no claim to " ultimate sovereignty." But the commission does not stop there. It goes on to make its opposition to all state totalitarianism explicit.

In a democratic community, the state makes no pretense to exercise political control over all the interests and phases of community life. Homes, schools, business, the press, churches — all have large areas of independent activity, not invaded by the state as long as they do not interfere with the maintenance of public order. In a totalitarian community, on the contrary, the state is in theory entitled to regiment all community interests and groups under complete political control. State and community in theory are coextensive. Such theory is antithetic to Christian belief.

Having thus thrown down the gauntlet to all totalitarian concepts of state authority, this commission of American theologians goes ahead to define the relation of God to the war, and of the church to the war. In brief, it may be said that, in respect of the former, it holds that God is on neither side in war, but that He takes sides " with the impulses toward good and against the impulses toward evil in every man and every group in both camps. God is not a combatant, nor a neutral onlooker, nor a helpless victim." The war is, in fact, God's judgment on man — not in the sense that God wills it (God does not will war any more than He wills slums or slavery) but in the sense that when men disobey or defy His will this judgment, this punishment, inexorably follows. " Man brings down punishment when he acts in violation of God's law made dynamic by God's will."

In other words, what the commission is here doing is cutting the church free from ideas so common in the past that a war is God's judgment *upon the enemy*, with the corollary that the state in which the church is located is God's agent to carry out this judgment. It is a measure of the steady approach of the church toward the Christian insights of the New Testament that not a whisper of this traditional idea remains in this report. On the contrary, there is repeated emphasis on the fact that all men and all nations must share in the responsibility for having thwarted the will of God and so brought this judgment on mankind.

Do conclusions such as these wake echoes in the minds of American readers? They should. For they parallel with startling fidelity the thoughts which were in the mind of our greatest American when he stood on the steps of our national Capitol that March day in 1865 to deliver his Second Inaugural. Listen to him again, wrestling with the moral and theological problems which the War Between the States had borne in upon his searching and sensitive soul:

Neither party expected from the war the magnitude or the duration which it has already attained. Neither anticipated that the cause of the conflict might cease with, or even before, the conflict itself should cease. Each looked for an easier triumph, and a result less fundamental and astounding. Both read the same Bible, and pray to the same God; and each invokes His aid against the other. It may seem strange that any men should dare to ask a just God's assistance in wringing their bread from the sweat of other men's faces; but let us judge not, that we be not judged. The prayers of both could not be answered — that of neither has been answered fully.

The Almighty has His own purposes. "Woe unto the world because of offenses! for it must needs be that offenses come; but woe to that man by whom the offense cometh." If we should suppose that American slavery is one of those offenses which, in the providence of God, must needs come, but which, having continued through His appointed time, He now wills to remove, and that He gives to both North and South this terrible war, as the woe due to those by whom the offense came, shall we discern therein any departure from those divine attributes which the believers in a living God always ascribe to Him?

Fondly do we hope — fervently do we pray — that this mighty scourge of war may speedily pass away. Yet, if God wills that it continue until all the wealth piled by the bondsman's two hundred and fifty years of unrequited toil shall be sunk, and until every drop of blood drawn with the lash shall be paid by another drawn with the sword, as was said three thousand years ago, so still it must be said, " The judgments of the Lord are true and righteous altogether."

" Both North and South . . . those by whom the offense came." " The judgments of the Lord are true and righteous altogether." Is this not the same thing the Calhoun commission is trying to say when it insists that all must share in the responsibility for having brought this judgment of war on mankind? But Abraham Lincoln said it eighty years before the theologians.

With regard to the relation of the church to the war the Calhoun commission is equally clear that, in loyalty to its God, it cannot become a belligerent on one side or the other. " The true church," it says, " cannot, and the institutional church ought not, act as a belligerent, not even as an unarmed cobelligerent, in any war." Because the church is a supranational body, it must not take part in any war " as though it were a civil community or a constituent part or a partner of a civil community." " In this sense," says the commission, picking up a phrase much used, and sometimes debated, in the American churches since Pearl Harbor, " the church is not at war."

Said the *Christian Century* in commenting on this section of the theologians' report:

In declaring unanimously that the church is not at war, the commission thus crystallizes and gives high expression to a conception which has only recently become current in Christian thought. Throughout Protestantism the uncritical assumption has prevailed that when the nation was at war the church was also at war, and always on the side of the nation. The churches regarded themselves as nationalist bodies, civil communities or a part or partner of such a community. They therefore blessed the nation's war banners and pronounced the sanctions of God upon the nation's cause. With the statement of the commission before us, we shall never go back to that un-Christian conception which allowed the church to identify itself with the nation in a manner which made God a tribal deity and denied the ecumenical character of the Christian community.

Then the editor, Charles Clayton Morrison, proceeded to this interpretation of the reasons which impelled the commission to its conclusion:

Among all the institutions of human society, the Christian church is unique. It derives its character from the God whom it worships. Its sole and inclusive mission in the world is to bear witness to the will of God as it has been revealed in Jesus Christ. This and nothing else is the church's reason for being. It bears this witness in many ways. . . . It is to bear this witness no less in wartime than in peacetime. Because its God does not will war or take part as a combatant, neither must the church be a combatant. Its task in time of war is to do in its human way what its God is doing. It must proclaim the divine judgment on the sins of which war is the " horrid fruitage," heal the wounds of battle and work in every way for a just and lasting peace.

In a later passage in the Calhoun report, this group of American theologians also raises the question of the relation of the church to the state through the institution of the army and navy chaplaincy. While they insist on the necessity for the church to carry on the spiritual ministrations of the chaplaincy to the men under the harrow of war — and so far as I know no serious exception was taken to this insistence even by the most thoroughgoing pacifists during the war — they warn that

the church is not a partner of any state, however loyal church members may be as citizens, and its ministries are offered not as civil duties but as the church's witness to a spiritual Lord of all mankind. Hence, we believe the church must persistently seek, on behalf of its ministers to men in the armed forces, both freedom from military restraints that hinder their work of Christian ministry, and clear recognition that they serve as clergy of the Church Universal rather than as officers of the several belligerent governments.

The relation of that concluding observation to the American system of commissioning chaplains as officers in the army and navy is so clear that the report adds: " Many of us believe that from the standpoint of the church, civilian status would be preferable to military rank for ministers in the armed forces." It will be of interest to see, during the next few years, whether this sentiment finds any echo among the ministers who have served as chaplains and the laity who have been under the ministrations of chaplains with officer rank in the recent war.

VIII

In this by far too hurried and sketchy manner I trust that I have made it clear how complete is the break between Leviathan at war and the Christian church. The state, any state, making modern war goes totalitarian because modern war cannot be successfully waged on any other basis. Even the passing of mass armies will not change this; states that must deal with the atomic bomb increase their controls over civilian activity to the most extreme limits conceivable. But the church insists that, even though the state has gone to war, the church is not at war, that it serves a God who is not a belligerent, that its only purpose in time of war is to do works of mercy, to uphold rights of conscience, to seek the bases of a lasting peace and to hold up the fact that this tragedy has been visited upon mankind as a vindication of God's justice. How is the church, how is the Christian, to give reality to this rejection of the claims of the state to entire control in wartime?

Traditionally, opposition to the operations of the war-making state has been pacifist. Individuals have refused to fight, believing that to be the commandment of the Christian law of love, and believing that by such " testimony " there will eventually be recruited a pacifist group sufficiently large to make it impossible for states to resort to war. A few churches have, as organized bodies, sought to withhold themselves and their members from martial service. There are Christians, and among them some of the most devoted and courageous spirits in the contemporary church, who believe that the pacifist witness contains the most satisfying and effective method by which to rid the world of the curse of militarism and recurrent wars. One cannot but be impressed, and given pause, by such lives. If I have arrived at another conclusion it is, let me admit, despite a frequent misgiving that I am taking issue with men and women whose shoe-latchets I am unworthy to loose.

Nevertheless, I cannot get away from the conclusion that, when Leviathan makes total war, the compromises which are then involved in any degree of pacifist " witness " less than prison or martyrdom are so obvious to the rest of the community as to make the claim of being a pacifist hardly more than an empty form of words. With the community making war, no man and no body of men can withdraw from the war without withdrawing from the community. The issue then no longer presents itself — as it largely did in a former day — as a relatively simple one of bearing arms or refusing to bear them. The issue is rather one of continuing to live in society.

The recent war disclosed very few pacifists who refused to make their contribution to the functioning of society, even though society was engaged in making war. Those who called themselves pacifists during the war often boggled at participating in certain direct war-making acts. They would not buy war bonds; they would not save tin cans or paper or kitchen grease. But there was no record of any significant number refusing to pay taxes, which would have been the one effective way of separating themselves from the war-making community.*

The pacifist of adult age whose " testimony " simply consists in occasionally expressing a vague regret that his country has gone to war, in abstaining from certain public acts in support of the war effort but likewise abstaining from any overt opposition to that effort, in agitation for an early and just peace — what effective difference is there between the " testimony " of this man and that of hundreds of thousands of soul-sickened Christians who would never think of calling themselves pacifists but who long for peace, pray for peace and work for peace up to the limit of their understanding and determination? As to the unsatisfactory nature of the " testimony " which is left to the pacifist of army age under conditions of total war, it is enough to point to the waves of frustration and unrest which passed over most of the camps for conscientious objectors during the war — so much so that one of the " peace " churches employed a distinguished expert in mental disorders to study the psychological difficulties which beset the Civilian

* If the number of pacifists in prison, mentioned earlier, be held to vitiate this conclusion, it must be remembered that in World War II the category listed as " pacifists " in federal prisons was more than half made up of members of Jehovah's Witnesses, who went to prison not because of any strictly pacifist scruples but in most instances because of a dispute with Selective Service authorities as to whether, under the Witnesses' conception of the ministry, they were entitled to exemption from military service on the same basis as the clergy of other churches.

Public Service selectees in camps under that church's direction.* And the heart-searching which went on in the peace churches with regard to the dilution of their " testimony " resulting from their cooperation with the war machine in conducting C.P.S. camps was of such a revealing nature that a non-pacifist observer who recognizes the noble motives with which the system was inaugurated feels under constraint not to comment upon it.

If I understand the nature of this modern world even a little, the fight against war must be of a different sort than a verbal and illusory abstention from the terrible business of war-waging after the war starts. Wars have to be stopped before they start. They have to be stopped by " doing away with the occasions of war." George Fox was right about that. But that means doing away with Leviathan. It means doing away with the social and economic injustice, the sense of political insecurity and the sense of personal frustration out of which Leviathan arises. It means doing away with the political irresponsibility with which Leviathan operates. The only pacifism which is more than a self-deceptive label is the pacifism which is out to do active justice, between the nations, between the races, between man and man, in the days before war starts. The Christian church can be effectively " pacifist " only as, before war starts, it stands up against every manifestation of the Leviathan spirit and purpose among the nations; only as it works for a social and political order which is in accord with the requirements of the moral law.

* Cf. " Conscientious Objectors: Their Morale in Church-Operated Service Units," by Anton T. Boisen. *Psychiatry: Journal of the Biology and Pathology of Interpersonal Relations,* August 1944.

CHAPTER IV

IMPERIAL LEVIATHAN

I

If the Christian church finds itself at greatest tension with the state when the state goes to war, it is in most continuous tension when the state goes imperialist. In the age of Great Powers, imperialism has become an accepted mark of power. Even a war ostensibly fought for human freedom has not noticeably diminished or weakened the imperialist structure. On the contrary, all the white empires, even though their inner weakness was revealed by the fighting, are being restored, except that of Italy, which is forfeited as spoils of war. And the self-proclaimed anti-imperialist giants which emerge from the conflict the principal victors now give promise of celebrating their victory by erecting two new empires — Russia in the form of satellite states all along its immense borders, and the United States in a network of " security bases " that will cover the Pacific and dot the Atlantic with American outposts.

This always threatening conflict between Christianity and imperial Leviathan might be avoided if the church were to give up its missionary ambitions. But as long as the Christian missionary insists on telling African blacks or Indonesians or the members of any of the innumerable castes of India that in the eyes of God they are of equal worth with their imperial masters, that they are entitled to equal rights and equal powers in the light of a gospel which knows neither Greek nor barbarian, bond nor free, just so long is the preaching of Christianity bound to have subversive effects and the spread of the church to undermine the foundations of the whole imperialist system.

The recent war, as a true world war, quickly drew into its orbit all the principal mission fields of the Christian church. The vast stretches of colonial territory that were fought over — in many instances twice, with invasion and counter-invasion — were areas where Christianity had been seeking its principal expansion for a century or longer. Where no actual fighting occurred, great armies from the so-called Christian nations, including the United States, were based, as in India and Iran. In addition, powers fighting for their lives made heavy drafts on colonial populations for fighting troops. England found Indian soldiers of enormous value in the Near and Middle East. France drew heavily on her African colonies. The United States has acknowledged its indebtedness to the Filipino guerrillas.

Were these colonial forces fighting to restore the imperialist system? They did not so understand. On the contrary, the war propaganda of the victors was designed to make the peoples of what are now euphemistically spoken of as " dependent areas " believe that victory for the Allies would be followed by a vast expansion of human freedom throughout the world. The Atlantic Charter, drawn up by President Roosevelt and Prime Minister Churchill in the summer of 1941 as the principal weapon in the Allies' arsenal of propaganda, and reiterated again and again throughout the course of the war until it was finally reaffirmed in the Potsdam Declaration which formed the basis on which Japan surrendered, made explicit promises:

First, their governments seek no aggrandizement, territorial or other.

Second, they desire to see no territorial changes that do not accord with the freely expressed wishes of the peoples concerned.

Third, they respect the right of all peoples to choose the form of government under which they live; and they wish to see sovereign rights and self-government restored to those who have been forcibly deprived of them.

But what the Atlantic Charter seemed to offer with one hand, the heads of the fighting nations, with one eye on their future imperial intentions, took away with the other. Mr. Churchill never succeeded, while he remained in power, in referring to the Charter without in some respect managing to throw doubt on its good faith. By the time he had finished "interpreting" it an Oriental might be forgiven for questioning whether, in the British view, it applied to any peoples other than those already in possession of its promised gains. Even his final reference in Parliament, in which he affirmed that "the Charter is as valid today as it ever was," lent itself to cynical interpretation.

Mr. Stalin formally adhered to the Charter in the impressive ceremony staged at the White House on January 1, 1942, but later denied its applicability to Finland, Poland and the Baltic republics on the specious ground that Russia had occupied these territories before it took the Charter pledge. With regard to that argument, William Henry Chamberlin pointedly comments: "As for the suggestion that the Charter is not retroactive, one need only consider the implications of its phrase about restoring sovereign rights and self-government 'to those who *have been* forcibly deprived of them.' The Charter was drawn up on August 14, 1941. What an international laugh would have been provoked if Hitler, on August 15, had announced that he accepted the Charter, but would, of course, retain all his conquests as of that date, because the Charter was not retroactive." *

But in some respects the most dismaying record of all has

* *America: Partner in World Rule.* By William Henry Chamberlin. New York: Vanguard Press, 1945.

been that of the United States. The President of the United States was, on the later testimony of Mr. Churchill, largely responsible for the Charter's formulation. What motives urged him to that action we shall perhaps never know. But in view of the circumstances it is not presumptuous to believe that one major factor in Mr. Roosevelt's mind during those August days of 1941 was the hope that such an avowal of idealistic purposes might weaken the evident reluctance of a majority of his countrymen to enter a " shooting war." Once in the war, the late President found the Charter of value mainly as propaganda to rally the support of the " billion potential allies " of Asia. Thus, on February 23, 1942, he declared: " The Atlantic Charter applies not only to the parts of the world that border the Atlantic but to the whole world: disarmament of aggressors, self-determination of nations and peoples, and the Four Freedoms." Twice later he was to reaffirm this assurance. And in addition, he must have authorized the speech delivered by his acting secretary of state, Sumner Welles, at the tomb of the Unknown Soldier on Memorial Day of that first year of America's participation in the war: " Our victory must bring in its train the liberation of all peoples. Discrimination between peoples because of their race, creed and color must be abolished. The age of imperialism is ended. The right of a people to their freedom must be recognized."

That was one side of the picture — the side which showed the United States trying, as a war strategy, to win the confidence of the colonial peoples. What was on the other side? An almost complete indifference to the actual moves made to restore the imperialist system, culminating at San Francisco when the American delegation took the lead in opposing the inclusion of any hope of " independence " in that part of the United Nations Charter which deals with the future of dependent areas. When the United States undertook the campaigns that were to make possible the return of Britain to rule

over Burma, Malaya, Hongkong and islands in the Pacific, of
Holland to rule over Indonesia, of Australia and New Zealand
to rule over islands in the Antipodes, of France to rule over
Indo-China, what stipulations did it make regarding a speedy
grant to these peoples of " the right to choose the form of
government under which they live "? None. When Ethiopia
pleaded for small parts of the two Somalilands to give that one
independent African kingdom a fair chance to develop economic strength, when Egypt sought to exchange her simula-
tion of freedom for the real thing, when Syria and Lebanon
tried to rally the moral opinion of the world behind their demand for the liberty promised them, what did the United
States, as author and champion of the principles of the Atlantic
Charter, do to help them? Nothing. Or at least, nothing that
shows on the record.

So far as the record goes, not only is there this negative attitude on the part of the United States, but the colonial peoples
have not forgotten the distressingly jaunty fashion in which
President Roosevelt, not long before his death, cast doubt on
the historical status and importance of the Charter. In one
of the most unabashed exhibitions of that opportunism in foreign relations on which he prided himself, Mr. Roosevelt dismissed the provisions of the Charter as no more than " aspirations " whose realization was not to be expected in any near
future. They were, he said, mere hastily jotted down mem-
oranda, of such a fugitive nature that no originals had been
preserved!

In thus minimizing the Charter's status — probably as a ges-
ture of appeasement to the two allies who, with the approach
of victory, were making clear their intention of writing a traditional victor's peace — the President stirred up a storm of
protest from the American people which evidently surprised
him. He hastened to declare that the press had misunderstood,
had misquoted him. He was as devoted as ever to the prin-

ciples of the Charter; they remained as much as ever the basis on which the United States and its allies were pledged to make the peace. But the mischief had been done. The levity of mind with which the Charter was regarded in high quarters had been revealed.

But why labor the case longer by commenting on the nature of the lip service subsequently paid the Charter in the Potsdam Declaration or by various leaders of the victorious Allies, including Stalin? The truth, now being uncovered by all the moves being made to liquidate the war, is that the Atlantic Charter is being dishonored both in letter and in spirit. The end of the war brought a mad scramble among the European victors to regain their lost empires and to divide the empires of the defeated. The " anti-imperialist " Soviet Union has come out of the conflict dominant over a greater empire than ever felt the power of the tsars. And the United States? The idealist, anti-militarist, anti-imperialist United States? Well, as this is written the definitive terms of peace are still to be made known. But already the United States finds itself in western Asia being drawn into the almost hopeless involvements of the situation in Palestine; in middle Asia it has already signed a guarantee of the future territorial integrity of Iran and seems intent on becoming deeply involved in the disposal of the oil deposits of Arabia and Ethiopia; while in eastern Asia, after putting an end to the Japanese empire, it has not only made a present of restored colonialisms to its European allies but, by its determination to turn the Pacific into an American lake, it has brought itself face to face with Russia across an imperialist chessboard where the next bloody move may be for control of the tempting prize of China.

All of which is to say that, despite the portent of the atomic bomb, the war has not ended the era of Great Powers. And a Great Power is drawn, by a historical compulsion that has never been denied, into the practice of imperialism. For Great

Britain, for Holland, for France the reasons are not far to seek. Without the restoration of their empires, such states could never claim the perquisites of a Power. England without her empire would be another Sweden; Holland another Norway; France another Spain. Mr. Churchill, in the days of his prime ministership, was too acute to mistake this and too candid to attempt to disguise it. General de Gaulle seems to be guided, in this respect, by the same lights that marked Mr. Churchill's course.

As for Russia and the United States, the case is even more tragically foreclosed. For them and in them the age of the Great Powers has come to its climax. They stand, at the close of the Second World War, the two supremely Great Powers. In some respects they are the only Powers to which the adjective should be applied. For they alone can pursue ends of their own devising without the necessity of seeking support from allies or collaborators. But great power breeds its own sense of great insecurity, great danger. Inevitably so, since the state thus able to impose its will on others knows how swiftly the frustrations, the privations, the humiliations of the lesser states will congeal in hatred, suspicion and plots against the mighty. Therefore the Great Power seeks to place its greatness beyond jeopardy by embarking on various imperialist adventures.

In Russia's case these are rationalized as the protection of a bordering ring of " friendly " satellites who can be depended on to throw themselves between the Soviet homeland and any attack. In the case of the United States the rationalization transforms an island empire possibly as far-flung as from the Azores to the Ryukyus, from the Aleutians and Greenland to New Caledonia, into nothing more than " security bases " whose place in the American scheme of things is so essential that no other nation is granted a right to take exception. Nevertheless, the result is two great empires, built by force, maintained by force, extending the area of master-slave relationships. Two imperial Leviathans — both wondering whether, as the Swiss historian, Jacob Burckhardt, predicted more than seventy years ago, the age of Great Powers is to reach its destined culmination in a super-crisis when even the two Leviathans are no longer content to divide the world, but join battle to determine which one shall rule in solitary power.

II

However, our purpose is not prophecy but analysis. In what way does the outcome of the war, with the revival of so many imperialisms and the threatened appearance of new ones, affect the relations of the Christian church with the modern state? The answer depends on two factors, neither of which can as yet be fully measured. It is possible, however, already to see how easily either of these factors may produce a condition in which the missionary church will be thrown into something closely approaching outright conflict with the imperialist state.

The first of these factors is the sense of betrayal, of having been deceived, held by colonial peoples. The second is the extent of the white Powers' determination to maintain their empires. How deeply does the native of a dependent area, longing for freedom, feel that he has been duped by the war propaganda of the Four Freedoms, the Atlantic Charter and the high-sounding speeches of the Allied leaders? To what limits are the empires prepared to go to preserve their claims to rule over subject peoples and territories? How much freedom, civil and religious, dare they permit? And hence, to what extremities of crisis must we expect the politics of Asia and Africa to be carried before there is a resolution of the demands of now dependent peoples for self-government?

As a missionary agency the Christian church must everywhere move within the limitations imposed by these questions.

For the church no longer seeks to present its gospel to naïve peoples who see the missionary in no social context other than that of the scriptural morality which he preaches and, to the best of his ability, exemplifies. On the contrary, it must do its preaching today to members of the tinted races who are as aware of the shoddy moralities of Western life as any Norman Thomas or Oswald Garrison Villard, who are as alive to the sense of desperation within Western society which has produced two world wars in a generation as any William H. Auden or T. S. Eliot, who are as cognizant of the failure of the Christian church to bring Western institutions under the control of Christian moralities as any Reinhold Niebuhr or Middleton Murry.

At the same time, the church in its missionary aspects cannot ignore the presence of existing colonial governments. If it is to work openly — and all institutionalized missions must work in the open — it must work under the conditions laid down by the imperial administration. If that administration comes into conflict with native aspirations for greater freedom (or it would be more candid to say, *when* it comes into such conflict) the missionary church must determine at what point its devotion to human liberty will require it to stand in judgment on the assertion of an alien control. Yet it can have no assurance that by withdrawing its sanctions from the imperial authority it will win for itself the confidence of the peoples struggling for freedom.

In such a situation, beset with grave perils on either hand, timorous counsels are certain to recommend a spurious neutrality as the mission's best hope of security and favor. It will be fraudulent advice, first, because there can be no such thing as neutrality in a struggle between an alien ruling power and a people's longing for freedom, and second, because evasion of the issue in its early stages will only insure a more bitter retribution when the day of popular triumph comes.

Let us, however, look at this issue in the immediate form in which the war has bequeathed it to the churches. What is actually to be the fate of " dependent areas " during the next few years? The United States has promised outright independence to the Philippines, and will undoubtedly make good on that promise not later than July 4, 1946. Whether it will do so on terms that presage something better than economic catastrophe for the islands remains to be seen. Great Britain has promised dominion status to India and some form of autonomy to Burma. Holland has promised the reorganization of the Dutch Empire, with autonomy for Indonesia. The provisional government of General de Gaulle has promised a reconstitution of the restored French Empire, so that its principal overseas components — Indo-China, Madagascar, the African colonies, those in the West Indies — shall enjoy a measure of self-government somewhat analogous to that of the British dominions. At the moment of writing (in late August 1945) it seems probable that these promises will be fulfilled in such a way that the people of the Philippines will be satisfied, and the people of India, Burma, Java, Sumatra, Malaya, Indo-China and Hongkong won't be.

No serious promise of change in the imperial system in Africa has so much as been made. There will be some division of former Italian colonies as spoils of war; it is not impossible that the United States may seek certain " security bases " on the west coast of Africa or on islands close to that continent. Russia for the first time has shown an intention of mixing in African affairs by her successful demand for a seat in the conference to dispose of Tangiers, and by the determination with which she has stuck to her effort to share in the disposal of Italy's former holdings. The only important proposal for any major alteration in the imperialistic pattern in Africa was that put forward by Field Marshal Smuts, prime minister of the Union of South Africa. In the famous speech in which he virtually invited the nations of western Europe to join the British Empire, General Smuts argued that control of colonies and mandates should be " devoluted " from the colonial office in London to the nearest dominions. But since this would mean, in actual practice, that the blacks of all the British colonies in Africa would be subjected to the brutally repressive race policies of the Union of South Africa, English liberals have felt it incumbent on them to oppose the Smuts proposal with all the vigor they could command. It can be assumed, therefore, that the imperial pattern in Africa will remain about as it was before the world plunged into a war that was supposed, to quote Sumner Welles again, to "bring in its train the liberation of all peoples."

Regarded as a whole, it is safe to predict that after all the conferences have been held and all the treaties written which fix the nature of the world left by the Second World War, it will be found that the imperialist system is going right on, much as it has been, with at least three major exacerbating factors continuing to operate within it:

First, there will be a continuation of the master-servant relationship inherent in ownership. There will be attempts to soften this, or to gloss over the realities by forms of words. Grants of limited power to local legislatures may seem to disguise some of the harsh facts of imperialism. But while ultimate control and power remains somewhere outside the country itself, the master-servant relationship is still there. That is why the British dominions insisted on the Statute of Westminster. That is why most of the current talk about the obligations of trusteeship toward politically immature peoples on the part of the white empires seems to the tinted peoples so much hypocritical eyewash.

Second, there will be a continuation of economic exploitation, as the peoples of the dependent areas define that term. I am aware of the arguments by imperialist apologists which seek to prove that colonies and mandates are a drain on the treasuries of the empires, and that it is really only as a sort of international charity that the colonial system is maintained. Yet as long as the control of the economic development of any area or people is held by others, and as long as the returns from that development flow principally to the coffers of others, the people of the region thus developed will regard themselves as exploited. India today furnishes an example, although almost any British publicist, if you bring up the matter, will at once begin to talk about how Britain is a debtor to India, and would almost make you believe that India, having profited so greatly at Britain's expense during the war, should now launch a lend-lease program to lift poor old England out of the bog of bankruptcy.

Third, there will be a continuation of color discriminations, enforced by the whites in colonial areas. It is not true to say, as frequently it is said, that there are no color lines drawn in French colonies or in Dutch. In some respects the lines are less hard and fast in Dutch colonies than in British and American, and they are still more relaxed in French. But they are there — and every black, brown and yellow man knows it. It is conceivable that the white may show a little more sense about flaunting his claims of color superiority after the experiences of the recent war, but I am by no means sanguine. I fear, on the contrary, that the very fact that he feels his empire system under pressure will make him the more insistent upon enforcing the social discriminations which advertise his claim to the right to possess and rule the empires. Only in Russia will you find a preponderantly white nation which honestly means to put into effect such promises as that of Sumner Welles which I have already quoted: "Discrimination between peoples because of their race, creed or color must be abolished."

III

Now all this makes trouble for the Christian churches on many fronts. The areas where the things of which I have been speaking, are happening, or seem about to happen, are areas within which the churches are seeking to carry on what they regard as their divinely ordained missionary activities. Moreover, they believe that never were such activities as much needed as they are now when, with the fighting ended, almost every traditional missionary method may be put to good use in bringing that rapprochement of peoples without which there can be no lasting peace. Although this is not the place to argue the question, I think it true that a more reasonable and convincing case for Christian missions can be made on the basis of the present postwar crisis than has been possible for many decades past. Nevertheless, there can be no escaping the conclusion that the continuation of the imperialist system will place upon the churches, in their endeavors to resurrect and expand their missions, almost unbearable handicaps. To understand why I say this, consider only three facts:

First, there is the fact, already mentioned, that the restoration of the colonial system will seem a betrayal of pledges or implied promises to practically all native peoples. Wendell Willkie had begun to worry about the effect of that fact on the future status of all Americans in the Orient, as readers of *One World* will remember. But the effect on the status of Christian missionaries is likely to be peculiarly distressing. For missionaries inevitably stand in the position of recommending an ethics, a morality, a philosophy of life which, if not presented as superior to all others, the missionary must at least regard as of very great worth. Otherwise, why does he try to carry it abroad? Yet the missionary can seldom, if ever, disengage himself from his national and cultural background. So it will come to pass, if the imperialistic system is restored and continued, that the Christian missionary in colonial areas will be seen against what the people of those areas regard as a background of broken promises and governmental deceit and immorality. Devoted charitable service on the part of individual missionaries may lessen the weight of this handicap, but it will never remove it. The effect upon the Christian mission, considered as a whole, is likely to be deplorable.

Second, and even more important, in the projection of its interests to colonial areas the church soon finds its efforts confused, if not confounded, by the marked divergence between its teachings as to the supreme worth of every individual, the wrong of exploitation and the iniquity of racial discrimination in the sight of God, and the actual practices of the dominant whites in the colonies. The antagonism felt by white traders and officials to missionaries has long been one of the stock appurtenances of plays, movies and stories dealing with colonial regions. It is no figment of the novelist's imagination. Sometimes this antagonism roots in personal factors. Not all missionaries are easy to live with. (And, I might add, not all traders or consuls are either.) But more often this antagonism roots in the situation, and its existence is in a way a tribute to the missionary. It grows out of the fact that, in so far as the trader or the representative of a banking combine or of a government is engaged in exploiting or repressing the people of these areas, to that extent he instinctively sees in the representative of the Christian church a threat to his own future. The missionary is, in the eyes of hosts of other whites in Asia and Africa and the islands of the seas, a trouble-maker. He is often accused of " ruining the natives "! Which is to say, in telling them that they stand equally well in the sight of God as any white man, the missionary puts ideas in their heads that finally come to fruition in all sorts of revolutionary movements. In this difficult situation, it sometimes happens that the missionary proves himself a white man first, an Englishman or an American or a Belgian or whatnot second, and a Christian emissary only third. But now the situation will be more difficult for the Christian churches than it was before the war, because in many colonial areas the period of missionary pioneering is about over and the church now depends for its leadership and expansion largely on an indigenous ministry which is under no temptation to twist the gospel into accord with the convolutions of British or American or Belgian or other Occidental prejudices. On this ground also, therefore, the church in a colonial region is about to find itself at increased tension with the imperialist state.

Third, any revival of the imperialist system will make trouble for the church because the whole weight of the tradition of the New Testament is on the side of freedom. I do not need here to go over the arguments as to the religious source of the democratic idea. They have all come to light again in the resistance which the churches of Europe have offered to the tyrannies recently bedeviling that unhappy continent.

The difficulty in which the church finds itself in a colonial region where the dream of freedom has taken possession of men's minds is well illustrated by the contrast between the status of the Christian enterprise at present in China and in India. There are many Christian missionaries, and more Christian pastors and teachers, in India who have shown their sympathy for the aspirations to independence which have found expression in the Indian National Congress party. On the whole, however, I think it fair to say that the Christian movement in India has tended to stress the Pauline injunctions about accepting constituted authority. Individual Christians here and there have made trouble for the government of India, but in the main the British have felt that they could rely on the Christian community as a source of support for the British rule. It is very seldom that you will hear a missionary whose field

is in India speaking in much criticism of the British colonial
regime.   Dr. E. Stanley Jones is so conspicuous an exception
as to prove the rule, and it is worth noting that, having come
to this country on furlough, Dr. Jones was denied a British
visa to return to India as long as the war continued. Most Indian nationalists, I find, tend to regard the Christians in India
as lacking in sympathy for the idea of Indian freedom.   The
result is a gulf between the Christian movement and the national leadership in that country which may produce tragic
consequences — both for the church and for India — if these
national leaders ever attain real control in their own household.

On the other hand, the missionary in China has been under
no pressure to act as apologist for a colonial power. At least
in this century, and to a considerable degree earlier, the Christian enterprise has given encouragement to every Chinese effort to make China's independence a reality and to build her
up for the great future in the Orient which should be hers.   As
a result, it is seldom that you will find a missionary from China
who does not believe himself to be *en rapport* with the Chinese
people, and for whom the Chinese do not show the liveliest respect.   The only notable exception is in the relations of the
Christians in China with the communist movement there, and
in that instance a special problem is created by the avowedly
anti-religious orientation of communism.   But even in that instance, it is not uncommon to find both missionaries and Chinese Christian pastors from the communist regions who have
cordial relations with the communists because the communists,
despite their ideological prejudices, have become convinced
that these Christians are truly seeking to help China advance
along the road to genuine freedom and strength.

For concrete evidence of the extent to which the Christian
church finds itself at tension with imperial Leviathan, consider the positions regarding colonialism adopted by the Cleveland Conference of January 1945.   This conference, called by

one of the principal commissions of the Federal Council of Churches, was participated in by practically all the important Protestant denominations of the United States. It met to consider the Dumbarton Oaks proposals for a new world league, and to make suggestions to the subsequent San Francisco conference of the United Nations, in the name of American Protestantism, for such alterations in the Dumbarton Oaks scheme as would justify the churches in supporting adherence by this nation to the new body.

One of the issues which caused the Cleveland Conference most searching of heart was the future of imperialism. In some way, the delegates believed, provision must be made in the United Nations Organization for clearly defined methods whereby the international body could protect the peoples of dependent areas against colonial maladministration and could see that they were given every opportunity to advance rapidly along the road to full self-government. On that issue, Dumbarton Oaks had been silent. Unanimously, with a lack of debate which made some observers wonder whether these spokesmen for the churches realized all that was involved, the Cleveland Conference resolved that the Christian churches have " a responsibility to champion " the " right to freedom " of all dependent peoples, and to " call upon our government and others: (1) to proclaim self-government as the goal for all dependent peoples; (2) where dependent peoples are ready for self-government to give it now; (3) otherwise to initiate progressive steps suitable for each area for achieving that goal; and (4) in the interim to provide that all such areas shall be administered under the supervision of world organization."

At San Francisco, where the American delegation had the benefit of the services of the chairman of the Cleveland Conference, John Foster Dulles, as its principal adviser, the churches were given a demonstration of the way in which governments, while giving lip service to principles championed by liberal and idealistic elements, can actually pursue reactionary and tradition-bound courses. At no point did the San Francisco conference so grievously fail to live up to the hopes of those who looked for an extension of human freedom under the new league as in its provisions for the treatment of dependent areas. While it would be possible to extract from the disappointing Chapters XI to XIII of the United Nations Charter (Articles 73 to 91) phrases which make a pretense of endorsing the general principles to which the churches had given their support at Cleveland, it was well understood among the San Francisco delegates that these words were only pious window dressing to conceal the actual intention of the victor nations to retain the imperialist system without significant change.

Every apparent gift of rights or hope for subject peoples in the Charter was carefully hedged by some weasel phrase meant to insure that colonial powers would go right on treating their dependencies as they pleased without regard to the UNO or its trusteeship council. Thus, the promise of developing self-government in Article 73, b, is accompanied by the emasculating words, " according to the particular circumstances of such territory." A later promise to " promote the political, economic, social and educational advancement of the inhabitants of the trust territories, and their progressive development toward self-government or independence," * immediately takes it all back by adding, " as may be appropriate to the particular circumstances of each territory " (Article 76, b). Since each colonial, or trustee, power is to be the judge of

---

* Nothing that happened at San Francisco was of more disquieting portent than the action of the American delegation in fighting to keep the word " independence " out of this article. It required an uprising of the smaller nations, led by the Soviet Union and forcefully aided by the delegate from the Philippines, to insert in this disastrously weak section of the Charter even this acknowledgment that independence may be an ultimate goal for dependent peoples.

what is " appropriate " in the territories under its control, the value of this promise is just about minus zero.

What territories are to be given even this equivocal protection against imperialist exploitation? Article 77 is so vague on this vital question in its vital clause — " It will be a matter for subsequent agreement [By whom? Under what conditions?] as to which territories in the foregoing categories will be brought under the trusteeship system and upon what terms " — that it is impossible to answer with confidence, but apparently only such territories will be included as the possessing powers choose to have included. And lest even this should not prove sufficient protection for imperial interests, the United States was instrumental in forcing the San Francisco gathering to write into the Charter a whole section, Articles 82 and 83, which provides for a system of " strategic areas," and is in reality just one vast hedge on the whole trusteeship principle, since it permits any Great Power to designate any territory it holds as a region which is, for military reasons, entirely out of bounds for inspection or consideration by the new league.

If space permitted, still other quibbles and escape clauses in the new Charter could be pointed out. Suffice it to say that by the time the trusteeship council gets through trying to make something out of the deliberate vaguenesses inserted in that portion of the Charter which defines its " functions and powers " (Articles 87 and 88), it can hardly be blamed if it asks whether it has any authority at all. And then, as if all this did not amply protect the imperial order against disturbance, the UNO wrote in the blanket exemption of Article 80, 1 — a provision so obviously designed to restore and retain the colonial status quo as it existed before the war that, on the insistence of the Soviet Union, the delegates were forced to add the pious admonition of the following clause, adjuring the imperialist states not to take undue advantage of the opportunities for denying the aspirations of dependent peoples which the first part of that article in the Charter had given them! *

The opening of this postwar period therefore finds the nations talking in vague generalities about increasing self-government for dependent peoples while seeing to it in actual practice that nothing is allowed to weaken their colonial controls or their unscrutinized administration of the regions in which they claim that they must maintain military installations. How great is the cynicism bred among Asiatics and Africans by this contrast between avowals and actual intentions hardly needs to be pointed out. These tinted peoples believe that developments at San Francisco gave the final proof, if more was needed, that the brave words about self-determination for all uttered during the war were no more than the strategic deceptions of hard-pressed combatants — another case of "when the devil was sick" — which now, with victory won, the victors have no intention of making good, and never did have.

What, in the face of this cynicism as to the moral good faith of the so-called "Christian" nations, and in the face of their own declarations on the imperialist issue, are the Christian churches to do? Are they to rationalize the decisions of San Francisco as "the best possible under the circumstances," and say no more about it? Or are they to go back to their Cleve-

* The portion of the UNO Charter in question reads as follows:

"Article 80. 1. Except as may be agreed upon in individual trusteeship agreements, made under Articles 77, 79 and 81, placing each territory under the trusteeship system, and until such agreements have been concluded, nothing in this chapter shall be construed in or of itself to alter in any manner the rights whatsoever of any states or any peoples or the terms of existing international instruments to which members of the United Nations may respectively be parties.

"2. Paragraph 1 of this Article shall not be interpreted as giving grounds for delay or postponement of the negotiation and conclusion of agreements for placing mandated and other territories under the trusteeship system as provided for in Article 77."

land demands for immediate self-government for the dependent peoples that are ready for it, name these peoples, and put all the pressure they can generate on the imperial masters involved to see this brought to pass? And are they to continue to insist that in other dependent areas there shall be set up carefully and publicly articulated programs leading by specified steps to the specified goal of self-government — Wendell Willkie's " firm timetables " on the road to freedom — while the whole colonial order of colonies, dependencies, trusteeships and strategic areas must be brought under the control and direct supervision of the UNO? If it pursues this latter course, then the church must expect to find itself at loggerheads with the imperial state over a large part of the area of its missionary operations.

IV

So we confront the question of the future of the Christian missionary enterprise. I have already indicated that, in my opinion, rightly conceived there is a greater need for and justification of that enterprise today than for years past. When I say " rightly conceived," I mean that the primary task which the churches will essay in sending out missionaries will not be that of listing converts to certain theological positions or adding to denominational rolls. Rather, the primary task will be that of trying to heal the wounds of war, to re-establish the sense of human solidarity across all boundary lines, to mediate the values of one culture to another (and by that I have in mind a two-way process), and to rally men of all cultures and nationalities to a supranational loyalty. Because the ecumenical church is the one institution which has preserved its ecumenicity through the war, it bears a special responsibility to undertake this latter task. I have just said that the church will not carry on its missions to gain converts, but in this sense it will. It will go after converts to the idea of an inclusive human brotherhood sharing an inclusive, supranational loyalty to a Divine Father of all, and to His Kingdom of Heaven which is above all the kingdoms of this earth and which men enter as they do His will.

Perhaps it will be widely agreed that this is the missionary task which lies immediately ahead of the Christian churches. But immediately one's sense of world realities begins to operate and one asks, How much of this sort of thing can be done? Actually, in such countries as Japan, or India, or China, or in practically all parts of Africa, how far can the emissaries of the church go without being, on the one hand, mocked by the nature of the society from which they come or, on the other, precluded from prosecuting their mission by the arm of government insistent on maintaining the status quo? I do not know. I fear that they cannot go very far without running into both these kinds of difficulties. But of course that in no way alters their responsibility, if they believe in the truth and saving nature of the Christian gospel, to push their mission to the utmost limit of their ability.

Of one thing I am sure. In the increasing tensions between the imperialist powers and dependent peoples roused to the hope of freedom, the Christian missionary enterprise cannot attempt to maintain a neutral position and survive. Where the issue involved is that of human freedom, the church cannot take the side of repression or slavery. If it does, it is doomed, not only because of the bitterness it will engender among the people to whom it is trying to commend the Christian gospel but even more because it has been false to that gospel. Yet this inherent propensity to encourage all efforts toward freedom may, under imperialism, create situations in which open missionary work will become impossible. The present strain which has developed between the Christian missionary societies composing the Foreign Missions Conference of North America and the British government over the pledge which missionaries and boards are required to give before they are permitted to work in India is a case in point.

For some years past — in fact, ever since the Indian nationalist movement began to assume impressive proportions after the First World War — all missionary societies of non-British incorporation or employing non-Britishers as missionaries have been required to give a pledge to the British government on behalf of their workers in India " that all due obedience and respect should be given by its members to the lawfully constituted government, in whatever part of India-Burma they may be, and that, while carefully abstaining from political affairs, it is its desire and purpose that its influence, insofar as it may be properly exercised in such matters, should be so exerted in loyal cooperation with government, and that it will only employ agents who will work in this spirit." Several American missionaries have been expelled from India for failing, in the eyes of the government, to keep this pledge. India is the only place in which the imperialist authorities exact such a pledge of support as the price of doing missionary work.

As can be easily understood, the giving of this pledge has been interpreted by Indian nationalists — of whom the most articulate and devastating has been Jawaharlal Nehru — as automatically lining the missionaries up on the side of a continuation of the imperialist regime. This matter came to a head at the annual meeting of the Foreign Missions Conference of North America, held in Toronto in January 1945. At that meeting the representatives of 125 mission boards operating from this continent, on a motion made by the representative of the Church of England in Canada, voted unanimously to ask the British to drop the requirement of such a pledge. If the British government refuses to do so, these mission boards then face the possibility of feeling a moral obligation to withdraw their representatives from India in order to seek to hold the confidence of the Indian people themselves. This, as I have said, is but one illustration of the growing tension between the churches and the imperialist state. But it is worth remembering that it involves one-fifth of the human race.

Those in touch with American church life know that at the present moment most of the major denominations are raising large special funds for postwar purposes. As I move about among the churches it seems to me that there is a widespread expectation that, by the proper employment of these special funds, a period of greatly expanded missionary activity may be launched as soon as mission fields are open for re-entry, in which the so-called overseas mission of the Christian church will reach a pitch of effectiveness never attained before. Although no one would put it so crudely, the idea behind many of these campaigns seems to be that all the churches need to do is to go out and get the money, and then their emissaries will be able to go out and get the converts. Sufficient generosity on the part of Western Christians will save the world for Christ!

I dislike to seem to be throwing cold water on any idealistic impulses, but all such ideas are not only sadly mistaken; they are capable of doing untold harm. It is going to take a lot more than money to get the Christian enterprise in colonial areas straightened away for productive service in this postwar period. In fact, the money element is going to be almost the smallest in the entire equation. The controlling issue is not going to be how many missionaries, but what kind of missionaries. By that I mean missionaries with what relation to the peoples of these colonies, and with what relation to the imperial authorities. To meet this problem it is quite conceivable that there should be no Occidental or Caucasian missionaries at all, or almost none.

In any event, the requirement at bottom will be to win again and hold the confidence of peoples who are all afire with the dream of freedom, yet who believe they are being denied

the fulfillment of that dream by the selfish interests of Occidental empires. Out of all the major mission fields, as I have
already indicated, China is probably the only one in which the
returning representatives of the Christian church will not have
to go clear back to that fundamental requirement and begin to
establish their status as true friends of the people all over
again. Until they do that, there will be such popular suspicion of their good faith and ultimate purposes as will render
all their good works ineffective.

There is one other and an even more taxing requirement,
which Christian emissaries from the West must meet before
they can regain the confidence of the dependent peoples.
They must prove their competence to examine the moral pretensions of the governments of their own countries and their
courage to hold these governments to moral accountability.
The atomic bomb has made this requirement inescapable. For
the Christian missionary the problem is not primarily that of
the awful destruction visited on Hiroshima and Nagasaki by
the two bombs which were actually dropped, although one
can hardly envy a pink-cheeked, starry-eyed young American
zealot who is commissioned by an American mission board to
go to Japan any time within the next decade and say, " I am
come in the name of brotherhood and good will to bring you
glad tidings from the Prince of Peace." But the problem for
the missionary is primarily that created by the apparent intention of the Great Powers to reserve the atomic bomb as a final
threat to impose the order and control that meets their wishes
on all the rest of the world.

With the atomic bomb in their arsenals, the Great Powers
need no longer care whether a world order of mutuality and
voluntary cooperation among free peoples is achieved. Indeed, the bomb simplifies the whole situation for the ruling
type of mind by making it unnecessary to bother with gaining
mutual consent. So long as possession of the bomb is confined

to the great states — and considerations of cost, technical equipment and available materials suggest that it is unlikely that small states will enter this competition for a long time — the Powers will be under almost intolerable pressure to conduct international affairs, as these affect small states and dependent peoples, under the easy formula, " This is our command. Before you dream of disobeying or defying it, remember that we have available the means to blow you off the face of the earth."

In other words, the arrival of the atomic bomb makes it necessary for the Christian missionary to work out a position on the use of power which shall meet the requirements of the moral law before he can hope to break down the suspicions and the cynicisms with which henceforth he will be greeted in the realms of imperial Leviathan. But to do this, as the missionary will quickly discover, will be to create immediate tension between himself and every diplomat, every trader, every financier, every soldier and sailor in a garrisoning force whose purpose is to keep the subject peoples subject, and to continue all those multifarious forms of exploitation that have made empire the goal of the nations.

Because I believe that the Christian missionary will see and measure up to these necessities which confront him — the necessity to side with the aspirations to freedom that he finds among the people to whom he would minister and the necessity to denounce the irresponsible use of power in the hands of the imperial state — I believe that we must expect increasing tension between the churches and imperial Leviathan. There are hard days ahead for Christian missions.

CHAPTER V

LEVIATHAN IN PEACE

I

In terms of philosophy and political science, as has been said, what we see today is a renewal of the struggle between Thomas Hobbes and John Locke. Both conceived of the state as the product of a social contract entered into by men intent on protecting themselves against the anarchy and insecurity of existence in what they called a state of nature. But whereas Locke conceived this contract as strictly limiting the powers of the state, and would grant to the state no authority which had not been clearly nominated in the bond, Hobbes regarded this contract as turning over practically all power to the state, to such an extent that he was ready to speak of it as " that mortal God to which we owe . . . our peace and defense." The watchword for Locke was freedom; the watchword for Hobbes was security. Locke's state had no reason for being except to insure for men their freedom to enjoy life, liberty and property. Hobbes's state was a great Leviathan to which men were ready to surrender all individual freedom in payment for the boon of order. Locke's effort was to protect men against tyranny. Hobbes's was to protect them against anarchy.

In the world of our forefathers, that fabulous eighteenth century out of which came the American Declaration of Independence and the French Revolution, John Locke clearly had the better of the argument. For the men of that period, liberty stood forth as the greatest of all goods, and any man who questioned that scale of values was regarded as either mentally retarded or an apologist for tyranny. Today, however, that judgment does not pass unchallenged. It is challenged not only in totalitarian states, but in many circles in democratic countries. The Lockian emphasis on liberty as the supreme value led directly to Jefferson's formulation of what has been called " Bill of Rights democracy " — the first ten amendments to the federal Constitution. But no less a champion of the common man than Henry A. Wallace has recently been insisting on the limitations of " Bill of Rights democracy," and suggesting that in totalitarian Russia Western democrats might find some useful hints as to the economic safeguards required by man living on this twentieth-century side of the industrial revolution. I gravely doubt whether there is in the Soviet state either the theory or example for the formulation of such a satisfactory economic bill of rights as Mr. Wallace evidently believes is to be found there. But that is beside the immediate point. The important fact is that Mr. Wallace's strictures on " Bill of Rights democracy " reflect a general and growing desire among contemporary men for a far greater measure of social security and order than they have hitherto known. If that involves giving increased powers to the state, so be it! The pendulum is definitely swinging away from Locke and back toward Hobbes and his Leviathan.

II

If there is any one thing of which modern man is convinced concerning himself it is his helplessness. And nowhere is this more true than of man in a modern democracy. A currently influential school of theology interprets the tragedies and difficulties of man's life in terms of man's pride, and sees in that pride the essence of his sin. One must acknowledge the penetrating character of many of the insights on which this particular theological thesis is based. Moreover, any observer can discover a lurking sort of what might be called mass pride among even the most bedeviled of our contemporaries. De-

spite their own admitted, and insisted upon, insignificance,
they gain satisfaction and a sense of status from the fact that
they are part of a *genus* that has weighed the stars and con-
quered the air and split the atom. Nevertheless, taken sepa-
rately, they are sure of their own helplessness. Any man who
has tried to stir his neighbors to attempt to clean up the scan-
dalous mess of most of our municipal politics will know how
pervasive is this sense. Nor is it confined to the undistin-
guished. Anyone who has attempted to secure support for
progressive legislation can testify that almost any congressman
will proclaim and bemoan his personal sense of helplessness at
Washington with as much conviction as your discouraged
neighbor in your home precinct.

The optimism which characterized the West as the present
century dawned has almost entirely disappeared. Ours is the
mood of Oswald Spengler; not of Herbert Spencer. And the
reason why our optimism has vanished is that it was so largely
based on the idea that, with the industrial revolution and the
development of technology, we were about to arrive at human
mastery through the machine. Today we ask whether in the
machine we have created a Frankenstein monster that will
ultimately destroy us. For all his amplified powers through
the machine, how much control over his own destiny does
modern man possess? Is he not rather as much as ever, and
perhaps more than ever, a pitiful creature at the mercy of the
working of impersonal forces which he cannot understand,
much less control? Hans Fallada's novel of the late twenties
expressed in its title a mood which did much to explain why
Germany finally embraced Hitler, but even more important
is the fact that it is now so much the mood of all the West —
Little Man, What Now?

One sees everywhere the evidences of modern man's inability
to understand, much less to control, his environment. It is a
fate which has befallen not simply the " little men," but those

who command our utmost resources of power. We all recall, for example, the spectacle which national leaders in all walks of life made of themselves in their efforts to explain to the public what was happening during the depression. The mere collection of their attempts at interpretation and at giving advice produced a masterpiece of sardonic American humor — that savage little book entitled *Oh Yeah?* And the evidence is clear that the men entrusted with government were quite as much at sea as all the rest of us. President Roosevelt battled with that crisis with a courage and unfailing nerve for which the nation should be eternally grateful. Nevertheless, the whole course of the Roosevelt administration came to be littered with the discarded initials of commissions, boards and other extemporizations that did not work.

There are those who now seem to find some sort of bitter inverted satisfaction in holding up against the memory of President Roosevelt the failure of the Warren policy of gold devaluation (that policy for which the London Economic Conference was scuttled), of the Keynes policy of pump-priming by deficit spending, of the policy of encouraging business revival by suspending the enforcement of key sections of the Clayton anti-trust act, of the NRA and the early version of the AAA and the WPA and all the rest. They point out that after pouring out almost fifty billions, Mr. Roosevelt still came down to the outbreak of the war with nine million unemployed, and that it took a world war really to end the American depression. It seems to me, however, that none of us has any reason to gloat about such matters. On the contrary, they should sober us as we reflect that even a man with the unexampled emergency powers possessed by the President of the United States, with endless resources of expert advice at his disposal, was able neither to diagnose the nature of the catastrophe which had befallen nor to control it.

If this was the experience of the most powerful man in the

world — for the President of the United States, when clothed
with the sweeping powers conferred upon him by Congress
while the emergency was at its peak, was just that — is it any
wonder that the commonality of mankind is increasingly overwhelmed with a sense of helplessness?

This helplessness registers in the mounting irresponsibility
of modern life which is having such destructive effects in society, in politics, in morals. We encounter this irresponsibility
everywhere we turn. How many stockholders in the United
States Steel Corporation, for example, have any sense of direct
responsibility for the labor policies of that business which they
own? To be sure, there have sometimes been one or two
shareholders who have turned up at annual meetings to challenge management policies at certain points. But they have
been regarded as amiable eccentrics whose principal service
was to provide the reporters with amusing incidents where-
with to embellish their accounts of otherwise cut and dried
proceedings.

About ten years ago a number of officials of American
churches, aware of the multiplied millions of industrial securi-
ties in the portfolios of denominational agencies, held a conference at which they discussed the moral responsibility of
church fiduciary agents in purchasing such stocks and bonds.
After several days of discussion, the only responsibility on
which they could agree was that church treasurers are morally
bound to see that the investments they make are financially
sound. Having talked all around and through the subject,
they threw up their hands at any attempt to work out principles of moral responsibility concerning the nature of the
business, or its labor policies, or its influence on government
or on foreign relations. The treasurer of a church board of
missions or of a church college or hospital, they agreed, is
morally bound to see that the church's investments pay their

interest when due. Beyond that they could not agree that the church as investor has any responsibility whatever.

It has become commonplace to say that the irresponsibility of the voter is digging democracy's grave. Yet I venture that 95 per cent of the readers of this book, if they voted at all at the last election, knew nothing and had done nothing to inform themselves as to at least half the candidates for whom they voted. Moreover, I doubt whether 10 per cent of the readers had participated in the processes by which those candidates got on the ballot in the first place. If there is condemnation implied in these observations, it applies to the author as much as to the reader. Well over half the candidates for whom I voted at the most recent general election were totally unknown to me; I had done nothing to influence the composition of the tickets submitted to the voters. The whole machinery of politics has become so complex, and therefore seems so baffling to most of us, that we are ready to leave its manipulation to the professionals.

Or consider the irresponsibility of the scientist for the results of his research. Nobel, who rationalized himself into a belief that his profitable invention of dynamite had made explosives so destructive that man would be forced to stop making war as a measure of self-preservation, is a symbol of the equivocal position in which the modern scientist finds himself. A Noguchi may attain martyrdom in the cause of human conquest of disease, yet his very discoveries may provide the basis for germ warfare. All over the world we are today witnessing the efforts of the scientists who produced the atomic bomb to dissociate themselves from any responsibility for the uses made of that weapon. They but put their talents, they insist, at the disposal of their governments. Patriots could have done no less. Responsibility for the result now passes to that amorphous entity, "society," which makes such a delightfully convenient repository for blame for all the troubles of mankind.

In this connection, how many have followed the social debate which has accompanied the final steps toward perfection of a mechanical cotton picker? Several machines for picking cotton are now all but ready for widespread commercial distribution. One of these, that invented by the Rust brothers of Mississippi, is reported to have been always a step in advance, technologically, of the machines which the great farm machinery companies have been developing. But the Rust brothers have been so oppressed by a sense of the social crisis which will be produced in the South when the cotton picker does away with the livelihood of the plantation workers that they have insisted that this machine shall be marketed only under conditions which have been cushioned against the shock, and that a large part of the income expected from sale of the Rust Brothers machines shall go into a foundation to alleviate the lot of the dispossessed cotton pickers. Now that the manufacture and sale of these machines has been taken over by a great industrial concern, the contract has been so drawn as to direct most of what would ordinarily be the inventors' profit into socially ameliorative channels. I am not sure whether the important point here is the unusual sense of social responsibility on the part of these inventors, or the fact that the rest of the farm machinery industry — and most of the South — looks on the Rust brothers as a pair of incomprehensible and more than slightly demented crackpots.

It is in this same area of general irresponsibility that we get what James Burnham has named our contemporary "managerial revolution." When society divides between impersonal ownership at one end of the line (and ownership tends to become increasingly impersonal, whether it is the ownership of huge corporations by thousands of stockholders or that of great industries by the state itself) with a horde of human sheep —

the " faceless masses " of Ortega y Gasset — at the other end, the way opens for the managers to step in in the middle and take over. Whatever one may think of the inferences drawn by Burnham, the fact of the rise of the managers can hardly be disputed. As Burnham uses that term, we can see almost everywhere this new élite. Governments of all kinds tend more and more to pass into the control of professional technicians — the " bureaucrats " of Republican campaign oratory — whose directives have far more to do with the actual business of running the country and its industries than do the laws passed by legislatures. Our vast industries are actually run by men who, in the words of a pamphlet recently published by the Machinery and Allied Products Institute, are " salaried careerists, to whom the company is simply a lucrative employer on a contract terminable at will." Or, as Pius XI put it in his most famous encyclical: " Immense power and despotic economic domination is concentrated in the hands of a few, and . . . those few are for the most part not the owners, but only the trustees and directors of invested funds, who administer them at their good pleasure." * Even the labor unions, after they pass through the first embattled days of organization, usually come under the direction of men who make a career of holding office in such organizations. As a result, most labor union members have only the most shadowy contacts, if any at all, with the men who make labor union policies, and Miami Beach fills up every winter with the labor union managers whose expense accounts make nothing of hotel charges of $35 a day. It might be possible to prove that there are even some churches which are actually run by a species of denominational manager.

This same growing sense of helplessness which makes the masses so ready to accept the services of the managers likewise produces a mass dread of the future. I am convinced that we

* *Quadragesimo Anno*, Part III.

here have to do with what may all too easily and quickly pass
into a mass psychosis which would have appalling effects. Of
the men whom the reader knows intimately — including himself — how many seem to have any deeply grounded confidence concerning the future? On the contrary, evidence
exists everywhere of the fears which dog the footsteps of all
of us. Consider, for example, the rush of today's college grad-
uates to get into what are known as " security " jobs — government berths, teaching positions with legal tenure, positions
in social agencies which can be sure that there will be no rapid
shrinkage in their " case load," posts on the staffs of research
and philanthropic foundations. Observers at the battle fronts
during the war agreed that the common anxiety of soldiers
was as to whether there would be good jobs enough to go
around when they returned; apple-selling was a nightmare
common to all of them. Such facts and tendencies when taken
together add up to puny man's sense of a need of salvation.
Where is he to find security? Where is he to find an end to
his fears? He turns to the state, and the state it is which answers: " Come unto me, all ye that are heavy-laden, and I will
give you rest."

III

For years this idea of state intervention to provide the goods
of life and security has been growing in fascination for Western man. It is not simply a product of certain types of European dialectical materialism; you can trace its rise as clearly
in the populism and trust-busting reformism native to our
American prairies. The omnicompetent state was, it may be
claimed, a dream of Marx and Engels. Yes, but it is just as
clearly foreshadowed in the pages of Edward Bellamy and
Henry Demarest Lloyd. So much has been accomplished by
government action to alleviate the ills of life and to develop
new sources of livelihood that the tendency has become gen-

eral to believe that if only the government is granted all power it can solve all problems.

This tendency to seek increasing power for the state has been accelerated by the idea of potential plenty in contrast with the experiences undergone by so much of the population during recent periods of depression and mass unemployment. Why should we be content with a society in which a third of the people are ill housed, ill clothed and ill fed while we have the potential resources to provide plenty for all? I am aware that this idea of potential plenty has been challenged by certain economists of note. Friedrich A. Hayek, for example, believes it " irresponsible talk " and quotes Colin Clark as saying in his *Conditions of Economic Progress:* " The oft-repeated phrases about poverty in the midst of plenty, and the problems of production having already been solved if only we understood the problem of distribution, turn out to be the most untruthful of modern clichés. . . . The underutilization of productive capacity is a question of considerable importance only in the U.S.A., though in certain years also it has been of some importance in Great Britain, Germany and France, but for most of the world it is entirely subsidiary to the more important fact that, with productive capacities fully employed, they can produce so little." Note, however, that the four countries in which it is admitted that there *are* periods of underutilization of productive capacity are the four in which the thinking of Western man is largely formed, and that this state of potential plenty in the presence of widespread poverty is acknowledged to form a genuine and characteristic problem for the United States.

Why, we ask, should so large a part of our population be subjected to such unnecessary hardships? The answer is customarily found in the economic injustice of our social order. Capitalism is equated with competition; competition with laissez faire; laissez faire with poverty in the midst of plenty.

To do away with the latter we conclude that we must get rid of laissez faire and bring a new order and control into the economic realm. We must shift from the pursuit of profit to an equitable distribution of the goods of life. That is what we commonly mean when we talk about the need for economic justice. And nowhere has there been a greater demand for economic justice in recent years than in church gatherings and among church leaders. Recent popes have been as insistent on this as such typical churchmen of other communions as the late Archbishop Temple, Bishop Francis J. McConnell, or the members of the Central Conference of American Rabbis.

But how is this equitable distribution of the goods of life to be achieved? Our first impulse is always to call on the state. Let the state step in to put an end to the dog-eat-dog competition of our rugged individualists; let the state see to it that production for private profit is turned into production for general use. The result has been the rise of the omnicompetent state. This began with the enactment of the first modest social security laws of a Bismarck and a David Lloyd George. But the development has been straight and swift to the emergence of the present Russian state and the concomitant forms of European totalitarianism. Did Hitler win Germany with dreams of empire? No, Hitler won Germany with promises of a state which would put an end to the unemployment of millions of Germans, a state which would protect the " little man " against the rapacity of what was defined as Jewish and bourgeois capitalism.

How is the state to produce this social order in which all men shall be secure against want and the dangers of unemployment? Here we reach the demand for " planning." Not planning, it must be understood, in the sense of using as much foresight as possible in a general approach to our problems of production and distribution, for this is simple common sense and is the course followed by every person of intelligence. But planning in the sense of giving the state all the power it requires to rule the entire economy according to some master plan drawn up by government, in which, as Hayek says, all the resources of society shall " be ' consciously directed ' to serve particular ends in a definite way." Or, if this be held the definition of an unfriendly critic, recall the words of that enthusiast for planning, Stuart Chase, who in *The Economy of Abundance* calls for " centralization of government; the overhead planning and control of economic activity. . . . The United States and Canada will fall into one regional frame; similarly most of Europe. Economically supreme over these frames must sit an industrial general staff with dictatorial powers covering the smooth technical operation of all the major sources of raw material and supply. Political democracy can remain if it confines itself to all but economic matters."

That last proviso is worth thinking about. For, as Walter Lippmann pointed out in *The Good Society:* " In view of the fact that schools, universities, churches, newspapers, books, even athletic sports, require money, marketing, and have to have economic support, the realm of freedom and democracy which Mr. Chase leaves is about equal to nothing at all." Implicit in planning carried to its logical conclusion, in other words, is the idea of state dictatorship, the omnicompetent state entering into and ruling every community and every life. Yet the fear of mass unemployment which has taken such hold upon the people of the West is today exerting an unremitting pressure toward the adoption of this conception of the responsibilities of the state and this policy of state action.

IV

However, despite the feeling of desperation induced by the specter of mass unemployment, the drive toward planned economies is by no means proceeding without opposition. Some of this, to be sure, comes from sources which are widely suspected of being interested in nothing but relaxation of *all* the controls which an often exploited society has placed on the rapacity of the profit-seeker. When certain industrialists raise the battle cry of "free enterprise," there are reasons to fear that the freedom in which they are really interested is the same freedom which lured on the "robber barons" of the second half of the nineteenth century.

But not all the opposition is of this nature. Perhaps the first book published in the United States seriously to raise the issue as to whether human freedom can survive under a planned economy was *The Good Society*, that book by Walter Lippmann first issued in 1937 and put out in revised form again only last year. Another was the book of essays by Albert Jay Nock, *Our Enemy the State*. Two books which have commanded much attention were written by the Austrian economist, Ludwig von Mises, now a teacher at Yale, *Omnipotent Government* and *Bureaucracy*. Still another pungent volume by that veteran pamphleteer, John T. Flynn, *As We Go Marching*, seeks to prove that the resort to deficit spending by any government in order to provide all the persons in a country with full employment will inevitably land any nation in the same sort of totalitarian tyranny as that in which Italy and Germany landed.

The most important study in this field is the book, first published in England and issued in an American edition last year by the University of Chicago Press, *The Road to Serfdom* by Friedrich A. Hayek. Hayek is also an Austrian economist who, after being forced to leave his native land by the rise of Hitler, has settled in Britain, where he is now a member of the faculty of the University of London. He writes with great solemnity and passion because, as he says, he sees countries like England and the United States, long the citadels of de-

mocracy, under the persuasions of planning entering on what
he declares are the same courses which led to the enslavement
of his former countrymen. It is the contention of Hayek that
as soon as the demand for planning as an end to economic
chaos reaches the point where it is necessary to determine
what *ends* are to be planned for, inability to reach agreement
by the public at large, or even by parliaments responsive to
differing and conflicting interests among the public, produces
a conviction that " if efficient planning is to be done, the direction must be ' taken out of politics ' and placed in the hands
of experts — permanent officials of independent autonomous
bodies."

" Planning leads to dictatorship," insists Hayek, " because
dictatorship is the most effective instrument of coercion and
the enforcement of ideals and, as such, essential if central planning on a large scale is to be possible. The clash between
planning and democracy arises simply from the fact that the
latter is an obstacle to the suppression of freedom which the
direction of economic activity requires. But in so far as democracy ceases to be a guaranty of individual freedom, it may
well persist in some form under a totalitarian regime. A true
' dictatorship of the proletariat,' even if democratic in form, if
it undertook centrally to control the economic system, would
probably destroy personal freedom as completely as any autoc-
racy has ever done." Because every man's life and work is so
entirely at the mercy of the national plan, what has been the
struggle for personal profit becomes an even more intense
struggle for control of the planning apparatus. Just how brutally ruthless this struggle can be recent Russian history has
shown.

It is the fashion in certain quarters to dismiss the warnings
which Hayek has uttered as the nostalgia of a conservative,
tradition-bound economist who wants to get back to stark
laissez faire, or else as the jitters of one not native to our Anglo-

Saxon tradition of democracy, who accordingly cannot understand our genius for providing democratic controls for processes which, in other societies, might indeed lead to despotism.

The first charge is palpably unfair. As John Chamberlain says: " Hayek is no devotee of laissez faire; he believes in a design for an enterprise system. Design is compatible with minimum-wage standards, health standards, a minimum amount of compulsory social insurance. It is even compatible with certain types of government investment. But the point is that the individual must know, in advance, just how the rules are going to work. He cannot plan his own business, his own future, even his own family affairs, if the ' dynamism ' of a central planning authority hangs over his head." Hayek himself says that he recognizes the need for planning in the distribution process; it is when the proposal is made to bring all production under a state plan that he takes alarm. For the necessity of keeping *all* industry to the stipulations of a national plan — or, in the vocabulary of NRA's Blue Eagle, to protect business against the chiseler — will, he warns, require such accumulations of police power that the final outcome will be a police state.

As to the second charge, Hayek simply does not believe that there *are* any democratic controls sufficient to keep a national or central planning system from dictatorial action. " There is no justification," he asserts, " for the belief that, so long as power is conferred by democratic procedure, it cannot be arbitrary; the contrast suggested by this statement is altogether false: it is not the source but the limitation of power which prevents it from being arbitrary. Democratic control *may* prevent power from becoming arbitrary, but it does not do so by its mere existence. If democracy resolves on a task which necessarily involves the use of power which cannot be guided by fixed rules, it must become arbitrary power."

However, the economic crisis may be so severe that the peoples of the Western democracies will choose to run the risks of state power rather than to suffer the tortures of mass unemployment. The British election which turned Mr. Churchill out of office furnished an illustration of this. In campaigning for a mandate to direct England's postwar recovery, Mr. Churchill placed his major reliance on what were, in essence, the Hayek warnings. A Labor victory, he trumpeted, would commit Britain to a socialized, hence planned, economy, to such an extent that both employers and workingmen would presently find themselves deprived of all real freedom and under virtual police control. To be sure, Mr. Churchill cast his election speeches in that highly metaphorical vein characteristic of his platform rhetoric, and thereby did his cause no good. Ordinary Britons simply would not believe that a government headed by Clement Attlee would introduce a Gestapo into English life, and it outraged their sense of fair play to have Mr. Churchill try to spread the idea that it would. Nevertheless, the election choice came to be essentially between a planned economy, as proposed by the socialists, and the Churchillian warnings against increased state powers of intervention and control in industry. On that issue the British electors rendered a verdict which should be taken to heart everywhere in the West.

The question which Western man confronts is this: If it be proved that industry under private control is not capable of avoiding the periodic disasters of the business cycle, and hence of protecting the masses against recurring periods of unemployment, can the state so order a national economy as to insure work for all at all times and at decent pay without assuming such dictatorial powers that individual freedom will vanish? The most thoroughly argued answer in the affirmative yet to be given has come from another British economist, Sir William Beveridge, the former head of the London School of

Economics and author of the " cradle to grave " social security proposals now before the British Parliament.   Sir William, in a book which faces the issue squarely in its very title, *Full Employment in a Free Society*, asserts that national planning for production as well as distribution is not incompatible with the personal liberties which Anglo-Saxons hold to be the necessary rights of free men.   How does Beveridge meet the Hayek challenge?

In the first place, Sir William draws a sharp line between what he calls " essential citizen liberties " and all others.   He is concerned to maintain only these *essential* liberties.   If the state must infringe on other traditional liberties in order to insure a successfully functioning economy at all times — success being measured by full employment — so be it.   So long as the essential liberties survive, the genius of Anglo-Saxon democracy is preserved.   What are Sir William's essential liberties? " Freedom of worship, speech, writing, study and teaching; freedom of assembly and of association for political and other purposes, including the bringing about of a peaceful change of the governing authority; freedom in choice of occupation; and freedom in the management of a personal income."   At first reading, this looks reassuring.   In the words of a song that my older readers will remember, " Who could ask for anything more? "

However, further exploration of the Beveridge scheme will show that there are various rights which he dismisses as nonessential which Englishmen and Americans in the past have deeply cherished.   Thus, he not only denies to the citizen the right to own any of the " means of production " or " to employ other citizens operating them at a wage " — rights which he contends cannot be essential since so small a portion of the citizenry has ever enjoyed them — but he also insists that the government which is to provide full employment must control all outlays, public and private, all investments, the location and nature of all business, what he calls the mobility of labor (by which he means that government agencies shall have the authority to tell all young people on leaving school into what occupation they shall go and to move all labor as required from districts in stagnation to where there is work) and that it shall control and distribute basic commodities.

What happens to labor unions in the Beveridge " free society "? Something, it is clear, not much different from what has happened to them in the Soviet Union. Theoretically, the right of unions to bargain collectively and to strike is preserved. But Sir William honestly admits that if the unions do not hold such rights " responsibly " — by which he appears to mean that they are seldom if ever to be exercised, but are to be suspended in favor of government arbitration of labor disputes — they will have to be taken away. Labor unions will no more be permitted to upset the government's industrial applecart in time of peace than they have been, in both Great Britain and the United States, in time of war.

Limitations such as these may leave what Sir William Beveridge regards as " essential liberties " unimpaired. Debate on that is likely to continue for some time. But what remains is hardly, despite the assurance of his title, a " free society " as that term has hitherto been understood in the Western world. It is, rather, a society planned and controlled in all its governing factors by an omnicompetent state. And the Beveridge candor is such that he makes it clear that if even this gigantic concentration of power in the hands of the state does not suffice to insure uninterrupted full employment, then, to attain that requirement of a stable society, there must be no hesitation about turning over to the state still other powers.

Here we face the dilemma of modern man. Confronted by the threat of recurrent periods of mass unemployment he declares that he can no longer endure the anarchy of competitive capitalism. But neither is he ready to subject himself to the tyranny of totalitarianism. A society without centralized economic planning has come to seem to him a calamity; he wants no more Great Depressions with their apple-selling and a WPA dole. A society with completely centralized economic planning has come to seem to him a monstrosity; there are few Americans or Britons who would reproduce at home the system which obtains in Russia. Instinctively, therefore, Western man is groping in all directions for the alternative to these two extremes, for the middle way, the compromise proposal which shall at one and the same time protect his livelihood and preserve his liberty. So far, it should be apparent, he has not made much progress toward finding it. Yet his search continues. In what directions?

As might be expected, there are calls for some system of democratically controlled national planning. Reference has been made to Hayek's belief that this is a mirage. Obviously the town-meeting technique is not adapted to the extremely technical task of working out schedules for national production and distribution. Lippmann warns that if Congress should try to initiate and control such planning in piecemeal fashion, thus hoping to bring the task within the measure of its comprehension, what it actually would bring about would be a repetition of the sad experience suffered in writing tariff schedules — a struggle between industrial interests (pressure groups) so politically potent that at last the whole scheme of planning would be reduced to a hodgepodge of special privilege and group concessions. The Labor party, on taking office in England, admitted this inability of a legislature to deal successfully with the formulation of a planned economy by announcing that it would rely, in carrying out its program of socialization, largely on directives issued by the permanent staffs of departments and by special commissions, rather than on acts of Parliament.

The first American attempt to secure something akin to a

national planned economy under democratic control is represented by a bill which, as I write, is before Congress. This
is S. 380 — the so-called Murray Full Employment bill. This
would empower the President annually to estimate the national production, savings, investment and employment for
the coming year. If these indices show that a boom period is
in prospect, then the President is to recommend to Congress
such a raising of taxes as will choke the movement toward inflation and provide funds for the reduction of the national
debt. (It is one indication of the new period into which we
have come that majority opinion now seems to approve government programs which may involve heavy deficit spending
without much concern over a national debt that, at 265 billion,
closely approximates the entire estimated national wealth. If
there is to be reduction of this debt, which in the days before
the war would always have been spoken of as " astronomical,"
this will have to come simply as a by-product of other government policies; few insist any more that debt reduction is a first
responsibility of a sound government.) But if the annual estimate warns that a depression, with mass unemployment, is
imminent, then the President is to recommend that Congress
(1) enact measures to stimulate expenditures by private agencies, state and local governments; (2) provide loans for small
business; (3) encourage private spending by lowering social
security taxes; and if all these fail to sustain the national employment level (4) embark on a federal program of public
works, using private contractors where possible, and paying
for the projects as far as possible from taxes.

It is too early to predict what the fate of the Murray bill
will be, although it is securing impressive support in its committee hearings. If adopted, it is even more difficult to predict
how its general principles will work in actual practice. One
wonders, in the light of experience, what the fate of such a
plan, involving as it does rapid shifts up and down in the fed-

eral tax structure, would be on the floor of Congress. How easily, or rather how quickly, could Congress be persuaded to accept the forecasts of the President's advisory commission as sufficiently dependable to justify the legislative action sought? In a matter of this sort, delay would be fatal; time is of the essence. Despite misgivings, however, if the government is in earnest about maintaining an economy of " 60 million jobs " (even though the 60 million, when no longer employed for slogan purposes, turn out to be 54) it seems probable that it will have to embark on at least as much of an experiment in planning as the Murray bill proposes. Whether this, when tested in action, will lead to the evils of log-rolling, pressure group competition for special privilege and outright graft that critics now predict, only time will tell.

American champions of the idea of democratically controlled national planning have one impressive argument on their side. Look, they demand, at the TVA! Has the nation not in that instance successfully carried through a democratically controlled plan for an entire region? And does not the success of this venture argue that the same thing can be done on a national scale without reducing the American people to a status where they are no more than pawns in the hands of Washington officials? As one who has been deeply interested in the Tennessee Valley Authority from its start, studied it closely and written on it rather extensively, let me say at once that I consider it the most hope-inspiring recent development in American life. If any of my readers are losing faith in the possibilities of democracy, I know no better tonic than the book by David E. Lilienthal published last year, *TVA — Democracy on the March*. We *do* have in the TVA a genuine measure of democratic participation in and control of a planning program. But this results from the decision of the TVA chairman, Mr. Lilienthal, rather than from the policy on which the Authority was organized. Left under its original chair-

manship, TVA would almost certainly have become as arbitrary and autocratic as any of the copper company satrapies in
Montana.

TVA is the sort of experiment in democratic planning it is
because Mr. Lilienthal is the sort of man he is. He has demonstrated that popular participation in planning is possible, at least
within regional limits. But it is worth noting that the plans
for other regional authorities now before Congress, although
presented to the public as " more TVA's," all place the authority in some department or bureau, or combination of ruling
boards, in Washington, and reject the very principle of local
autonomy and direction which Mr. Lilienthal believes has been
the secret of TVA's significance. So far as the issue of human
freedom within a planned economy is concerned, all the various so-called TVA bills now before Congress or in process of
formulation turn their backs on the Lilienthal experience and
propose to place the direction of future economic development in the Missouri Valley, the Columbia Valley and so on
in the hands of technocrats in Washington.

No, TVA is no guarantee that a planning system in a democracy will be democratically conducted. It is a *hope* that it may
be so administered; it is a *proof* that it can be so administered.
Yet the " authority " idea which has gained such favor in the
United States because of the TVA achievement, and the analogous " public corporation " scheme which is so widely supported in England, both carry within them the threat of an
increased control by agents of the central government over
the most ordinary and necessary concerns of the masses. Nor
does talk of the possibility of a " mixed economy," part planned
and part left to private enterprise, afford much reassurance in
this respect.

The difficulty with all proposals for a mixed economy lies
in deciding where the line of necessary government control is
to be drawn. How much of the nation's economy can be left

subject to the operations of private industry if the stabilized employment purposes of the planned portion of the economy are not to be wrecked? The more the " planners " consider this, the smaller grows the area for individual enterprise. Consider the revealing statement by that stalwart of liberal economic journalism, Stuart Chase, in his recent *Goals for America*, that a national planning system in a mixed economy need control only what he calls a Big Five of essentials: " adequate food, shelter, clothing, health service and education." Only these five? But when account is taken of all that is involved in providing these five for all of us, it is hard to see what will be left of importance in our lives outside the control of the government planning bureaus.

v

Does it need to be argued that the problem which is involved here is one about which the Christian church should have deep concern? The whole Judeo-Christian religious tradition is based on the affirmation of the inestimable worth of the individual in the sight of God. The one thing upon which Christian doctrine of all schools has agreed is that men are to be treated as ends and not as means. This position, which Nicolas Berdyaev developed again with such power in his recent book, *Slavery and Freedom*, is the Christian position as held by all churches and all schools of theology. Christianity is never in any doubt as to its relation to the *theory* of state totalitarianism. As the Calhoun commission of theologians put it, the totalitarian " theory is antithetic to Christian belief."

But in the growth of the demand for a planned economy to provide all men with economic security the churches face a condition and not a theory. Their humane sympathies are aroused by the exposed and insecure position in which so large a part of our Western society finds itself. Yet widespread uneasiness is created by such warnings as I have referred to against the totalitarian developments implicit in state planning and control. And this uneasiness is accentuated by the sight of the actual fate which has overtaken individual freedom in such nations as have adopted a planned economy in peacetime. The Protestant churches have not yet started a genuine search for alternatives to this regimentation. They have not yet seriously raised the question as to where the beneficence of the " social service state " turns into the tyranny of an omnicompetent Leviathan. Granted that they do not wish to see man left at the mercy of a return to the irresponsible " free competition " of a former period, and that they equally do not wish to see him become a slave to a totalitarian dictatorship, what is the alternative that the Protestant churches, as churches, favor? It would be hard to say. Movements such as those which Dr. James W. Fifield is fostering out of Los Angeles, and which Dr. Norman Vincent Peale is rumored to be about to project out of New York, seem to have little to offer save a reassurance to the conservative element in the community that not all Protestant church forces are committed to socialism. But where is the affirmative, constructive alternative, whether to socialism or to a return to unbridled laissez faire? What, to be candid, is Protestant thinking in this field offering beyond generalities and warnings?

It is my impression that in this respect Roman Catholic thinking is doing better. Not only is the mind of Catholicism concerned with the social dilemma in which modern man finds himself — most of the notable papal encyclicals, from *Rerum Novarum* of 1890 down to the present, deal with this issue of the relation of man to the state and to the securing of an adequate and stable livelihood — but it is at least trying to think its way to an *affirmative* position as Protestantism gives small signs of doing. Even the best Protestant deliverances, such as that which came from the Malvern Conference in 1941, seem to ooze out into pretty thin generalities when laid alongside the concrete Catholic proposals for, let us say, the development of a corporative state.

It is the fashion, I am aware, to dismiss all discussion of the corporative state idea by claiming that it is only another name for fascism. Anything that a communist, socialist or leftist intellectual does not like nowadays is pretty sure to be labeled fascism. Mussolini set up a fascist state; Mussolini announced that he had organized his state on the corporative pattern; therefore, the corporative state must be fascist. Thus runs the argument. But it is fallacious. The fact was that Mussolini's corporatism was never more than a paper scheme, drawn up long after his fascist state was a functioning actuality, and used only for window-front purposes of deception and propaganda. Mussolini's Italy never became a corporative state in any sense approximating that in which recent popes have used the term. There is no necessary link between fascism and the sort of corporative state envisaged, for example, in the " Program for Social Reconstruction " adopted by the bishops of the American Catholic hierarchy in 1919.

What is the Catholic proposal for a corporative state? Harold E. Fey, in his recent revealing series of articles * on the present program of the Roman Catholic Church in this country, thus quotes Monsignor Francis J. Haas (now bishop of Grand Rapids) in speaking before a " Catholic Conference on Industrial Problems " at the time he was head of the federal Fair Employment Practices Committee:

. . . Under this system all employers, workers, professional persons — all — would be organized. They would elect representatives from their respective industry or profession to deal for them, and these representatives with government representatives guiding them but not dictating to them would in actual practice operate the industry or profession. Thus the direction of the system would be tripartite. The representatives would be chosen

* Cf. the *Christian Century*, Dec. 27, 1944.

from each of three categories — management, workers and government.

Each industry. For example, all the personnel, employers and employees alike, in the textile industry would through their freely elected representatives and *with the guidance but not dictation of government*, determine wages, hours, prices in the textile industry and work together for its common good. The same would be done in steel, transportation, agriculture and all the rest. Finally, all the industries and professions would be linked together on a tripartite basis in a national body. This national body would be made up of representatives of management and workers from the industries and professions, with the government sitting with them *as guide and friend and not as dictator*. The purpose of this national parliament would be to maintain, so far as it can be done, proper balance in prices and wages among the various industries and professions.

Note the clauses in this speech by Bishop Haas which I have italicized. You may think what you will of this as a program, but at the very least you must admit that it seeks to offer a specific alternative to economic chaos and insecurity for the masses on the one hand, as well as to government dictation on the other. This program the Catholics claim to derive almost in its entirety from the *Quadragesimo Anno* encyclical issued by Pius XI in 1931 in commemoration of the fortieth anniversary of Leo XIII's *Rerum Novarum*. In this remarkable document, which on the whole I regard as the most important *official* declaration issued by any Christian church in this century, the pope gave clear evidence of his benevolent interest in the corporative state idea. This he described in these terms:

The state here grants legal existence to the syndicate or union, and thereby confers on it some of the features of a monopoly, for in virtue of this recognition, it alone, according to the kind of syndicate, can represent workingmen and employers, and it alone can conclude labor contracts and labor agreements. Affiliation to the syndicate is optional for everyone; but in this sense only can the syndical organization be said to be free, since the contribution to the union and other special taxes are obligatory for all who belong to a given trade or profession, whether workingmen or employers, and the labor contracts drawn up by the legal syndicate are likewise obligatory. . . .

The corporative organizations are composed of representatives of both unions (i.e., of workingmen and employers) of the same trade or profession, and as true and genuine organs and institutions of the state they direct and coordinate the activities of the unions in all matters of common interest.

Strikes are forbidden. If the contending parties cannot come to an agreement, public authority intervenes.

Little reflection is required to perceive the advantages of the institution thus summarily described: peaceful collaboration of the classes, repression of socialist organization and efforts, the moderating influence of a special ministry.

This is not to say that the pontiff placed his seal of approval on the corporative society as the only one meeting the Roman Catholic ideal. As a matter of fact, *Quadragesimo Anno* proceeds to acknowledge certain misgivings in the papal mind: " It is feared that the new syndical and corporative institution possesses an excessively bureaucratic and political character, and that, notwithstanding the general advantages referred to above, it risks serving particular political aims rather than contributing to the initiation and fostering of a better social order." This, it should be borne in mind, was written in 1931. Could Pius XI have had Mussolini's " corporatism " in mind? He certainly could!

But no disappointment with corporative experiments, in Italy, in Portugal, or elsewhere, has convinced either Pius XI or his successor, the present pope, that the church does not have an economic and political order in the corporative system which it is justified in recommending to the state as a means of escaping from communist dictatorship on the one hand while on the other insuring industrial peace and a rewarding standard of living for all workers. So committed is the present pope to this principle that, according to Mr. Fey, " he would have the same principle of representation used in setting up the controls for international economics." It is worth noting that the pope thus commits the Roman Catholic Church to some international system of economic organization.

It must not be supposed, however, that Catholic interest in the search for a new social system is confined to championship of the corporative state. Many Catholic thinkers and church authorities, especially in the United States and Canada, apparently are looking in still other directions for the means of bringing about such revisions in the social order as recent popes have declared necessary. Especial significance attaches to the discussion of the potentialities of the cooperative and distributist movements which goes on incessantly in Catholic periodicals and at conventions of various Catholic societies, particularly those dealing with rural life. The cooperatives developed around St. Francis Xavier University at Antigonish, Nova Scotia, have become almost a shrine to which flock American pilgrims looking for an alternative for capitalistic competition. And nowhere is there more intelligent interest being shown in proposals for taking the factory worker back to the land and breaking up the huge concentrations of productive power in cities than among Catholic sociologists. When Pius XI in *Quadragesimo Anno* pilloried the factory system with the memorable words, " Dead matter leaves the factory ennobled and transformed, where men are corrupted and degraded," he gave all Catholic thinkers the signal to undertake a search for a constructive alternative. Increasing numbers of them believe that they have found it in decentralism. And many industrial leaders are beginning to give the decentralist thesis serious consideration. Henry Ford has started to decentralize his vast industrial empire and — what may prove more important in advertisement-conscious America — has begun to publish magazine advertisements pointing to his first thirty experiments in decentralization as essays toward a new and better way of life. Other industrial giants, the United States Steel Corporation among them, are reported to be contemplating other experiments of the same nature.

By thus stressing the Catholic interest in finding a constructive alternative for monopoly capitalism on the one hand and human regimentation on the other, I do not mean to imply that Protestants are indifferent to these issues. Intelligent criticism of the present social order has been characteristic of most Protestant assemblies ever since the turn of the century. The "Social Creed of the Churches," a Protestant document, gives evidence of fully as deep a concern for the welfare of the worker as is to be found in *Rerum Novarum* or *Quadragesimo Anno*. Individual Protestants are conspicuous in the cooperative movement, in decentralist agitation and in the experiments in new types of community organization that are to be found in many parts of the country. Nevertheless, the impression persists that official Protestant approach to these issues — that is to say, by denominational action or in the plenary sessions of interdenominational bodies, such as the Federal Council of Churches — has been largely negative in character. There are innumerable official Protestant denunciations of the injustices suffered by the common man under capitalism. But there are few, if any, Protestant parallels to the actions of the pope and of the American hierarchy in giving affirmative approval to a specific alternative.

What should Protestantism support? If it believes that modern man, left at the mercy of the competitive struggle for private profit, will be subjected to such insecurity and want that, for self-protection, he is under temptation to deliver himself a captive to the Leviathan state, then what has it to propose as an alternative? It must make up its mind soon, for Western man has come to the point where he will act. If he believes that the postwar economic collapse feared by many prophets of doom is about to engulf him, he will make some choice *now*, not in the next decade or the next generation. Accustomed as years of war have made him to live under the compulsions of a state planned and controlled economy, he will choose a return to those same controls rather than face the prospect of idleness and hunger. It is time, therefore, for Protestantism to cease laying all its stress on the failures of the capitalist order, and to point toward a way of salvation.

What is that way? It is not my purpose to try to answer that question in this book. To attempt to do so would require a book of its own. Perhaps I may venture to put my beliefs in such a book some day. But now it is enough for me to say, without elaboration, that I hold that the social order most adapted to the needs of Western man, if he is to be assured a sufficient livelihood, a sense of the worth of his industry, a genuine measure of control over his life and work, an environment in which his capacities will have fullest opportunity to develop, and freedom in accord with his noblest traditions, will be one in which the principles of cooperation, decentralism and the single tax are combined.* But I have no desire to argue any such program for a reorganization of society here. All I am trying to establish here is that, if the Protestant churches mean to have any constructive part in pointing Western man to a security which is other than the security of a police state, they have not long in which to make up their minds what sort of social organization they believe in and to go into action to prepare the way for it.

Despite any opposition from parishioners who may think they have a stake in the preservation of the status quo, despite

---

* I include the single tax because I am convinced that, without it, it is impossible to solve the tragic problem of inadequate housing. Other plans for government housing, or subsidization of building enterprises, simply add to the control of the omnipotent state over the lives of its citizens.

the tremors of that type of church functionary whose first commandment, as Halford E. Luccock long ago pointed out, is "Thou shalt not upset the applecart," the time has come for the Christian church to take a leading part in the search for a social order which will safeguard the liberty of all men while it lays upon them and their governments a greater measure of responsibility to the general good than has been recognized under laissez faire. The church must stand at the forefront in guarding against too great a concentration of powers in the hands of the state. It must oppose Leviathan in peace as in war. It must do so because only free men can have a free church. And only a free church can preserve the moral health of society and of the state itself.

But this requires a far more serious search for an alternative to the present social order in the West than the Christian church has so far undertaken. For unless there is soon forthcoming the pattern for an achievable order that will offer men security and opportunity as well as freedom, Western man in despair will continue to commit his life and destiny more and more wholly into the hands of the state. The omnicompetent state, Leviathan in peace, constitutes a threat to man's freedom, not because hosts of thoughtful men do not see the danger and fear the state's concentration of powers, but because they do not see any alternative except those other tyrannies of industrial anarchy, of threatening starvation, of encompassing frustration.

CHAPTER VI

RELIGIOUS LIBERTY

I

Too few in the West, and especially too few Americans, realize what importance the problem of religious liberty is taking on for our day and generation. When one speaks of religious liberty your typical American thinks of Luther and the Reformation, or of William Penn and Roger Williams, or of Thomas Jefferson and the first article in the Bill of Rights — at any rate, of " old, forgotten, far-off things, and battles long ago." The truth is that religious liberty was never more at stake than now. For while on the one hand the rise of the totalitarian state has intensified the issue for all who cherish human freedom, on the other the church (and the synagogue as well) has a new perception of the peril in which it stands from all enhancements of state power.

Religious liberty is in danger today in non-Christian and Christian countries alike — in Moslem Egypt and Shintoist Japan as in Protestant Germany and Roman Catholic Spain. The threat to religious liberty comes as close to our own doors as Quebec and Durango. As an editor of a church weekly it sometimes seems to me that we never send an issue to press without having to record a new instance of religious intolerance or persecution somewhere. Religious liberty is nowhere nearly as widely established as most Americans believe, and it is everywhere in danger where other civil liberties are in danger.

In considering the struggle for liberty of conscience and of worship which is intensified by the encroachments of the modern state, I do not profess to present the results of original research. Fortunately, it is not necessary to do so. The research required to comprehend the dimensions and complexities of this problem has been done. Under the auspices of the International Missionary Council, Professor M. Searle Bates of the University of Nanking, China, has published one of the most impressive examples of research to come from church scholarship in recent decades.* For some time to come it is unlikely that there will be important additions or revisions of fact to be made to the Bates investigation. With the permission of Dr. Bates and of the International Missionary Council I have drawn heavily on this material in preparing this chapter, and I wish not simply to acknowledge my indebtedness but to register as well my admiration for a scholarly achievement of the first rank.

II

What is the present status of religious liberty? From the legal standpoint, according to Bates, there may be distinguished five categories of states in respect of this problem.

First, states whose constitutions or laws promise essentially full and equal religious liberty. There are 34 of these: Albania, Australia, Belgium, Brazil, Burma, Canada, Chile, China, Cuba, Czechoslovakia, Ecuador, Estonia, France, Germany, Guatemala, Honduras, Hungary, India, Japan, Latvia, Liberia, Lithuania, the Netherlands, New Zealand, Nicaragua, North Ireland, Palestine, the Philippines, Salvador, South Africa, Switzerland, Turkey, the United States and Uruguay.

Second, there are nine states whose laws recognize the preponderance of one religion, but which in principle assure satisfactory liberty for others: Bulgaria, Colombia, Eire, Haiti, Panama, Poland, Portugal, Syria and Yugoslavia.

* *Religious Liberty: An Inquiry.* New York: International Missionary Council, 1945.

Third, twelve states have an established religion, but their laws assure liberty for other religions without serious discrimination. These are Argentina, Bolivia, Costa Rica, the Dominican Republic, England, Irak, Paraguay, Peru, Scotland, Thailand, Transjordan and Venezuela.

Fourth, fifteen states have an established religion, and their laws grant that religion important privileges while discriminating against all others. The fifteen are Afghanistan, Arabia, Austria, Denmark, Egypt, Ethiopia, Finland, Greece, Iran, Italy, Norway, Rumania, Spain, Sweden and Tibet.

Fifth, two states are placed in a final category as opposing or restricting religion in general — Mexico and Russia. " Relaxation from furious anti-clericalism against a hated religio-political system," says Bates, " is now the order in both countries, but no new constitutional or quasi-constitutional crystallization appears either to have been reached or to be unmistakably at hand." Yet so far as the constitutions and laws of Mexico and the U.S.S.R. are concerned, they seem to grant quite as much religious liberty as obtains in countries which stand well toward the top of the Bates chart.

In considering a listing of this sort it must be borne in mind that all too frequently the legal basis for dealing with issues of religious liberty is one thing, and actual practice another. Some states which must be placed in the most favorable categories so far as their legal provisions are concerned have in practice found all sorts of ways for making the exercise of what we would regard as untrammeled liberty of conscience all but impossible. Bates distinguishes, after making all allowances, 21 such states: 7 Moslem by tradition (Albania, Turkey, Syria, Irak, Transjordan, Afghanistan and Iran); 6 Roman Catholic (Belgium in the case of the Belgian Congo, Colombia, Peru, Portugal especially in the case of her colonies, Poland and Mexico — why he does not include Spain I do not understand); 3 Orthodox (Yugoslavia, Rumania, Russia); 1 Protes-

tant (Germany under the Nazi regime); and 4 that fall into
no single classification (Japan, India, Burma, Thailand).

To conclude this attempt to chart the contemporary situation, consider one more of Bates's classifications, this time according to actual practices as distinguished from constitutional
or other legal provisions. Again there are five categories:

First, 30 states are credited with a high degree of freedom
from preferences and discriminations between churches and
religions: Australia, Belgium, Brazil, the British colonies, Canada, Chile, China, Cuba, Czechoslovakia, Ecuador, England,
Estonia, Eire, France, Guatemala, Honduras, Liberia, Lithuania, the Netherlands, New Zealand, Nicaragua, North Ireland,
Panama, the Philippines, Salvador, Scotland, South Africa,
Switzerland, the United States, Uruguay.

Second, there are 7 states in which preferences and discriminations are said to be relatively minor (Bulgaria, Costa Rica,
the Dominican Republic, Weimar Germany, Haiti, Hungary,
the Netherlands East Indies) and 11 in which there are important preferences and discriminations, but these not of an
acute nature: Argentina, Bolivia, Denmark, Finland, the
French colonies, Latvia, Norway, Paraguay, Sweden, Venezuela, Yugoslavia.

Third, Bates distinguishes three groups: (a) countries where
freedom of religion is limited in certain regions, with important social pressures — Anglo-Egyptian Sudan, Burma, Ethiopia, India, Nigeria; (b) countries where freedom of religion
is limited, with weighty preferences and discriminations —
Austria, Belgian Congo, Colombia, Mexico, Peru, Poland, Portugal, the Portuguese colonies, Thailand; (c) countries where
freedom of religion is limited, with state controls or state effort
on behalf of religion or quasi-religion — Nazi Germany, Italy,
Japan. It will be seen that there are 17 countries in this classification.

Fourth, 12 states are named in which freedom of religion is

severely limited, with state restrictions or socio-religious pressures heavy, or both: Albania, Egypt, Greece, Iran, Irak, Palestine, Rumania, Russia, Spain, Syria, Transjordan, Turkey (also certain India states).

Fifth, in three states there is no religious liberty, but death or utter ostracism is the penalty for apostasy: Afghanistan, Arabia, Tibet (also British Somaliland).

To see the issue as it really exists today, let us look at the situation in a selected group of countries.

Throughout Islamic lands, as Dr. Bates's lists indicate, the conception of religious liberty can scarcely be said to exist. In theory, at least, the condition has been achieved in the Moslem states which some Christians hold up as the ideal to be sought where Christianity is the dominant religion, as justification for a state church system. That is to say, under Islamic law, state, community and church are one. In only four Moslem countries is there any legal method of recognizing conversion to another faith. In many, converts to Christianity lose all inheritance rights, and frequently social pressure is strong enough to deprive such converts of their livelihood.

In Afghanistan and Central Arabia, as has been shown, conversion to Christianity is punishable with death. (It is interesting to remember that Ibn Saud, the most fanatical ruler of Saudi Arabia, after Yalta became the " great and good friend " of President Roosevelt, the champion of freedom of religion.) In British Somaliland intolerance is so fierce that Christian missions are not permitted by the British authorities. In Tripoli, so long as the rule of Fascist Italy continued, Mussolini called himself " the Defender of Islam," and pledged that " no attempt to convert Moslems to Christianity would be authorized by the Italian government." The single Protestant missionary there, a doctor, was expelled.

The difficulties which have beset missionaries in Iran have been too many to list, and even though reform tendencies have curtailed the influence of the Moslem clergy in the lower schools, and Christian schools have made a strong appeal to upper class families, the teaching of the Bible in Christian schools — or in any schools of general curriculum — is prohibited. However, there is general agreement that a greater measure of religious liberty can be enjoyed in practice in Iran than in any other avowed Moslem nation.

There is a guarantee of religious liberty in the Egyptian constitution, but the restrictions imposed render that of small effect. Not only is Islam the established religion, but Christians must submit their legal matters, such as those concerning marriage, divorce and family rights, to Islamic courts, while permits for building churches or holding religious services, which are a prerogative of the crown, are passed on by Moslem officials. Missionary work has become increasingly difficult in recent years, as the government has issued regulations designed not only to keep all Moslem students from being exposed to Christian teaching in mission schools but requiring that Christian schools shall teach Islamic doctrine to all Moslem students, using Moslem teachers and following a government syllabus.

Turkey, as one result of Mustapha Kemal's revolution, has abolished the caliphate, separated state and church, and set up an entirely secularistic government. The present Turkish constitution provides that " no one can be disturbed on account of the religion, rite or sect to which he belongs, nor for the philosophic opinions which he professes. All ritualistic ceremonies which are not contrary to the public order or morale, or inconsistent with the law, are authorized." The constitution also speaks of the present Turkish state as " laicist and revolutionary." As a matter of fact, this secularizing tendency is carried so far that it is against the law to have religious instruction of any sort in private schools, or any places of worship in such schools, or any members of religious orders on the staffs of such schools. Islam is taught in the lower schools, but attendance is optional. The difficulties thus created for Christian missionary work are obvious, but they are almost equally great for any active sort of Islamic propaganda. And it should be noted that the Bible and Christian periodicals can be freely circulated and sold in Turkey — something not true in most of the Moslem world.

What is the situation in Roman Catholic countries? We will begin with Spain. It is hardly an exaggeration to say that, except for the brief period of the republic, modern Spain has known no religious liberty. So complete has been the monopoly of the Roman Catholic Church, so stern the repression of dissent, so fully has the maintenance of the church and its privileges become identified with the preservation of the privileges of the reactionary ruling elements, that liberalism in Spanish terms has become practically synonymous with anti-clericalism and even anti-Catholicism, and the recent civil war tended from the start to be interpreted as a struggle between atheism and the Christian faith. Unfortunately, the Christian faith had a sorry set of champions in Franco and his Moors, his bloody-handed generals and his Nazi and Fascist allies.

The Catholic effort to picture the Spanish republic as an enemy of religion, because of the policy which established religious liberty, abolished the state subsidy for religious societies, broke the church monopoly on cemeteries, legalized divorce, dissolved the Jesuits and fixed firm controls on other orders, was hardly convincing to any outside observers except those who wanted to be convinced. It did not convince all Spanish Catholics. It seems much nearer the truth to say that the republic, at least at the start, wished only to follow the practice of other European states where the establishment of liberal political regimes had led to the disestablishment of the papal church — France is an example — and that there were many good Catholics among the republicans who honestly believed that the church, if disestablished and forced to seek its support on the basis of its service to the community, would be purified thereby and gain immeasurably in spiritual power.

However, the papal authorities refused to countenance any such interpretation of the purposes of the republican government, the pope (in his encyclical *Dilectissimi Nobis* in 1933) declaring " a spiritual war " between the Holy See and the republic and placing at the top of his list of eight charges against the republic the separation of church and state as " a most serious error."   As the civil war finally was fought there were horrible atrocities on both sides, and the Catholic Church suffered dreadfully in the torture and murder of priests and the destruction of property.   Sixteen thousand priests, monks, nuns and lay workers are said by the Spanish bishops to have been murdered and twenty thousand churches destroyed or looted.   Discounting the partisan nature of this report, the actuality was undoubtedly terrible enough.   On the other hand, there can be no question that the Franco forces committed unspeakable atrocities.   Yet the pope, in a broadcast on April 16, 1939, glorified Franco's victory as a victory for religion, saying: " Peace and victory have been willed by God to Spain, which now has given to proselytes of the materialistic atheism of our age the highest proof that above all things stands the eternal value of religion and of the Spirit."

The actual situation now obtaining in Spain is this: a concordat has been signed with the Vatican which provides that Catholicism is to be the sole religion, all others being excluded; that the church shall have control over all education and that Catholicism shall be taught in all schools; that the government shall accord all honors to bishops and Catholic clergy and shall support them in all their efforts against the perversion of the faith of the people; that the government shall not interfere in any way with the bishops or clergy in enforcing ecclesiastical discipline.   The government has a hand in choosing bishops and they must take an abject oath of loyalty to Franco. But the church has been given back all its old properties and prerogatives; the religious orders are restored to all their former power; the church is again financed by the state; all public officials and members of the armed forces must attend mass; all prisoners, including the thousands who still rot in prison after capture in the civil war, must attend mass; publication or circulation of the Bible is prohibited; of the 166 Protestant churches which existed a decade ago under the republic only two are known to be open now, and these are for the use of foreign groups living in large exporting centers.

In other words, with the downfall of the republican regime and the return of a situation in which she could fix the conditions of religious life, the Roman Catholic Church in Spain has shown that what she wants is not religious liberty at all but a complete religious monopoly. It should be added, however, that almost any Spaniard, of whatever political or religious coloration, will assure you that if Spain ever has another revolution (and most Spaniards seem to take it for granted that there will be another revolution before long), the treatment that will be accorded to the Roman Catholic Church will probably be even more severe than that which it experienced in the last civil war.

The issue takes another form when one crosses the border from Spain into Portugal, but in certain respects the situation there regarding religious freedom is even more significant than in Spain. Portugal is held up by many Catholic writers as the best existing example of a Catholic state, which though authoritarian in form under the virtual dictatorship of Premier Salazar, nevertheless closely approximates the social standards set by recent popes. There is today no established church in Portugal; in theory entire religious liberty obtains. The country is so overwhelmingly Catholic, however, that the issue hardly arises within Portugal itself as to whether other forms of religion would, if they sought it, be granted full freedom of worship and proselytization.

Under the terms of the concordat signed with the Vatican in 1940 (the most recent and therefore the most significant of the concordats) the Roman Catholic Church obtains innumerable rights and privileges. Exemption from taxation for church property and clergy is carried to astonishing lengths. There is no civil marriage, and no divorce. The church has almost entire control over education, though there are public schools as well as church schools — the latter subsidized by the government. Says the concordat: " The Catholic religion and Catholic morals will be taught in public elementary, complementary and intermediate schools to pupils whose parents or guardians have not lodged a request to the contrary."

It is in respect to the Portuguese colonies, however, that the issue of religious liberty becomes acute. The situation there is controlled by a " Missionary Agreement " with the Vatican signed at the same time as the concordat. What it works out to is a program virtually to force all Protestant missions out of Portuguese colonies, and to impose such disabilities on natives who may attend Protestant schools or join Protestant churches as effectually to discourage them from so doing. Catholic missions are subsidized by the government; land is given them free; buildings are sometimes provided; tax exemptions are so manipulated as to aid Catholic and to hinder Protestant work; Catholic missionary bishops are paid and pensioned by the state; so are Catholic missionaries. The Roman Catholic colonial authorities frequently refuse to recognize the validity of Protestant marriages.

In large measure this discriminatory policy grows out of the fact that according to the Portuguese constitution, Portuguese Catholic missions are recognized as " an instrument of civilization and national influence," or, as Premier Salazar expressed it in the speech in which he explained the concordat to the

National Assembly, there had been obtained by this deal with the Vatican a " nationalization of missionary endeavor, which is definitely identified with Portuguese colonizing action." In other words, Roman Catholic missions in Portuguese colonies are supported by the Portuguese state as an avowed agency of Portuguese imperialism.

But the policy has other practical results. In a recent article Dr. Emory Ross, executive secretary of the Foreign Missions Conference of North America, who probably knows more about the missionary situation in Africa than any other living American, directs attention to " the non-issuance of entrance visas for Protestant missionaries" to Portuguese colonies. " One large American board with sixty years of work behind it," writes Dr. Ross, " has for four years been unable to get a single visa from Lisbon for the entrance of its missionaries into Portuguese Africa! Efforts through our own appropriate government channels have so far remained fruitless, despite the fact that Portugal is in the category known as ' friendly nations' and that no specific objections whatever have been raised to the missionaries for whom visas have been asked." *

In view of all these disabilities it is hardly surprising that Protestant missions in Portuguese colonies are everywhere losing ground, and Protestant missionary leaders are everywhere apprehensive lest they shortly disappear entirely. This despite the fact that Portugal is a signatory to several international treaties which guarantee religious freedom in colonial areas. Portugal's own Colonial Act specifies that " the state shall insure in all its overseas territories liberty of conscience and the free exercise of the various religions subject to the restrictions necessitated by the rights and interests of the sovereignty of Portugal, the maintenance of public order and consonance with international treaties and conventions." But all such guarantees have not been worth the paper they were

* *Christian Century*, Jan. 3, 1945.

written on since the negotiation of the " Missionary Agreement " with the Vatican in 1940.

A parallel case exists with regard to Belgium, although we
do not have space to go into it here. It must suffice to say that
while the Roman Catholic Church holds the favored position
one would expect in Belgium itself, there is general religious
freedom there. But in the Belgian colonies all sorts of discriminations are in force, the object seemingly being to bring about
the eventual withdrawal of Protestant missions. Protestant
converts in the Congo are frequently confronted with the
choice of Catholic baptism as the only way of becoming el-
igible for teaching and other public positions to which they
may aspire.

Thence we turn to the much discussed subject of religious
liberty in Latin America. Here again it may be said that in
most cases the laws or constitutional provisions guarantee what
is spoken of as religious liberty. But in many of these countries
the actual practice is something else again. In addition to the
disabilities widely imposed on Evangelicals, both missionaries
and national adherents, Protestant missionary leaders believe
there is a concerted effort on the part of the Roman Catholic
hierarchy in this country and in the South American republics
to hinder further dispatch of Evangelical workers from the
United States. For a detailed consideration of this whole matter, the reader may be referred to George P. Howard's book,
Religious Liberty in Latin America?, or the even more recent
volume by Wade Crawford Barclay, *Greater Good Neighbor
Policy*.

Here, briefly, is a résumé of the situation within the various
Latin American countries. In Argentina Catholicism is declared by the constitution to be the state religion, religious
education by church-approved teachers is compulsory in primary and secondary schools, the Roman Catholic Church has
many kinds of special privilege and the Virgin Mary is carried

on the army rolls as an honorary general. Bolivia provides state support of the Catholic Church, but guarantees religious liberty. A good deal of unofficial persecution of Evangelicals by priests is reported from rural districts. Brazil has a good record on religious liberty — so much so that the government has been upbraided by Roman Catholic authorities for religious indifferentism. Chile guarantees and provides religious liberty. Colombia has a constitutional guarantee of religious liberty, but Catholic clerics control the schools and many kinds of disabilities are imposed on Evangelicals. Costa Rica supports Catholicism as the religion of the state, but there is general religious liberty. Cuba has complete religious freedom. The situation in the Dominican Republic is similar to that in Costa Rica. Ecuador has a good record in this regard. So has Guatemala.

Haiti recognizes " a special situation " for the Roman Catholic Church, but there is general freedom of religion. The Pentecostal Church was suppressed a few years ago, allegedly for disturbing the peace, but has been allowed to resume its work. Honduras has complete separation of church and state. Mexico likewise, but the Roman Catholic Church has by no means accepted this policy of the revolutionary government as representing a final decision. At the present time there are increasing reports of outbreaks directed against Evangelical churches and individuals in different parts of the country. Nicaragua has official toleration for all sects, but the record of local priests is bad. Panama recognizes Catholicism and provides for state support of the church, but there is general toleration. Paraguay also proclaims toleration, but Roman Catholicism is the state church, the archbishop is chairman of the Council of State and the foreign minister is a Jesuit. Peru has perhaps the worst record in Latin America, reaching a climax early this year when non-Catholics were forbidden to carry on services outside their already established churches.

Mass is celebrated every morning in all public schools, with required attendance. Salvador has religious liberty. Venezuela guarantees religious liberty in its constitution, and there is little or no official infringement, but the Catholic Church has a privileged position in the schools and there are many reports of attacks on Evangelicals, most of them from rural districts.

Take conditions such as these into account, then add the apparent intention of the Roman Catholic hierarchy to insist that Latin America must be considered as a closed Catholic preserve, not to be entered by Evangelical missionaries, and it is easy to understand why religious liberty in most of this continent is so seriously circumscribed.

Lest it be thought, however, that this represents the universal condition within contemporary Catholic states, reference should be made at once to Eire. The constitution of the Irish Free State " recognizes the special position of the Holy Catholic Apostolic and Roman Church as the guardian of the faith professed by the great majority of the citizens," but also " recognizes " the Protestant and Jewish bodies and contains these guarantees:

Article 44 (2) 1. Freedom of conscience and the free profession and practice of religion are, subject to public order and morality, guaranteed to every citizen.

2. The state guarantees not to endow any religion.

3. The state shall not impose any disabilities or make any discrimination on the ground of religious profession, belief or status.

4. Legislation providing state aid for schools shall not discriminate between schools under the management of different religious denominations, nor be such as to affect prejudicially the right of any child to attend a school receiving public money without attending religious instruction at that school.

5. Every religious denomination shall have the right to manage its own affairs, own, acquire and administer property, movable

and immovable, and maintain institutions for religious or charitable purposes.

6. The property of any religious denomination or any educational institution shall not be diverted save for necessary works of public utility and on payment of compensation.

Dr. Bates quotes C. J. Cadoux, the British scholar whose championship of the Protestant position makes his testimony especially convincing, as writing in his book, *Roman Catholicism and Freedom*, that " these conditions seem to have been on the whole honorably observed in the Free State, so far as the government, even that of Mr. De Valera, is concerned. Protestant schools, for instance, are generously treated, and Protestant judges are numerous."

Any full discussion of this issue would, of course, have to take into account the situation in Italy, in Germany, in Russia and in Japan. In each, I hardly need say, religious liberty has suffered grievous infringements, and at times has hardly existed at all. But in each the situation at the moment is so much in flux, dependable information is so hard to obtain, and the chances are so great that there will be major changes for the better (except perhaps in the case of Russia, where, it should be noted that so well informed though critical a commentator as David J. Dallin intimates in his recent book, *The Real Soviet Russia*, when Stalin has consolidated the gains of the war and is no longer avid for support from all possible sources of national unity he is likely to swing Soviet policy back into its old anti-religious orbit) that I pass them by.

Neither will we pause to note the restrictions on religious education which have been written into the laws of China, promising seriously to curtail missionary work in that country in the future if they are not repealed; nor the drastic curtailments on missionaries recently put into force in Ethiopia. Both these developments are not without significance, however, as indications of the possible effect of an aroused nationalistic consciousness in resolving to take no chances with foreign cultural infiltrations which might, in time of crisis, prove part of the imperialistic design of a foreign power or powers.

It is necessary, however, to remind ourselves before leaving this phase of the subject that there is no religious equality, and sometimes there is undeniable religious disability, in certain Protestant countries with the state church system. We need not here go into the arguments by which the maintenance of state churches in England, Scotland, Holland and the Scandinavian countries has been defended. I think I am familiar with most of those arguments, and I may add that I am entirely unconvinced by them. I believe that it would be better for the state, better for the people, better for the church, better for the cause of religious liberty, better for the cause of vital religion, and better for the cause of the Kingdom of God if in every instance these church establishments were disestablished. But that is not what I want to discuss now. All I want to do is to point out that religious freedom is at least to some extent compromised in these Protestant countries, as well as in the Moslem and Catholic countries we have been talking about.

Is there religious liberty in England? The question will sound absurd to many. Yet the Church of England is not free, as its clergy and members found out as recently as 1928 when the House of Commons — containing at that time several avowed atheists and one Hindu — refused to allow the church the right to change its own *Book of Common Prayer*. With the agreement of the entire House of Bishops of the Anglican Church, the Archbishop of Canterbury thereupon issued a solemn statement asserting the right of the church " to formulate its faith in him [Jesus Christ] and to arrange the expression of that holy faith in its form of worship." But though the archbishop and the bishops thus tried to assert their right to freedom in this regard, Parliament denied that claim, and there the established church stands today. It is not even free enough to fix its own order of worship! To be sure, individual congregations and parsons do so, but that is only because of the English genius for lawbreaking.

Likewise, as we all know, the Church of England does not have the right to choose its bishops and archbishops. An overwhelming majority of the present bishops of the Anglican Church have been chosen for their high office by a Unitarian, a Congregationalist, a freethinker, a Presbyterian, and a Welsh dissenter of one of those innumerable chapel sects that almost defy classification but which are closer to the Disciples than to any other of our American communions. It is probably true that the Church of England could have full liberty tomorrow at the price of disestablishment. But even though many of the leaders of that communion, including the late Archbishop Temple, have advocated disestablishment, the church itself has never shown any readiness to take that step. If disestablishment comes in England, as it has in Wales, the determining impulse will have to come from the state. I will not go into the question as to whether England enjoys religious liberty in the matter of schools, though for all I know there may be embattled Baptists over there, like wonderful John Clifford, who still spend their day a year in gaol for refusing to pay taxes to support schools run by the established church.

No one will deny the large measure of religious liberty that exists in the Scandinavian states. Adolf Keller tells of the incident when King Gustaf visited Spain some years ago and was thanked by the papal nuncio for the liberty which Catholics enjoy in Sweden. In his reply the king expressed his regret that he could not say the same thing for his Protestant brethren in Spain! But the Jesuits are excluded from Norway; the Baptist and other " free church " groups take exception to certain taxes which they regard as a penalty for nonconformity; and in all these countries the theory of virtual identity between the community, the state and the church is carried to such

lengths that not only does the king name bishops and Parliament manage the temporal side of the church's affairs, but the
Lutheran catechism is taught in the lower schools under conditions which make it very difficult for the ordinary family to
have a child released from such enforced indoctrination, and
the process of " including oneself out " of the state church —
to use a Hollywood phrase — is so involved and in many communities exposes the seceder to such obloquy, that thousands
stay in the state churches just because it is so much simpler to
stay than to get out.

If space permitted something should be said about the limitations on the liberty of the Orthodox churches in the Balkan
states which have resulted from their relations as establishments
of tyrannical and frequently corrupt governments, or the limitations on the liberty of the free churches in those same countries — the most outrageous instances having occurred in Rumania.   And there are further, and often distressing, problems
connected with the denial of religious liberty to minorities —
which is simply one part of the total problem of dealing justly
with minorities.

It is, I believe, fair to say that in most Protestant nations, in
some of the Orthodox world and in China this issue of religious
liberty does not occur in forms as repellent as it does under
every form of totalitarian state and in most Moslem and many
Roman Catholic countries.   But before jumping to the conclusion that it is impossible for either Moslem or Roman Catholic countries to grant religious liberty to a degree sufficient to
satisfy the liberal conscience, it is well to reflect that the most
recent constitutions written in a Moslem and in a Roman Catholic state grant practical freedom of worship and of conscience.
I refer, of course, to Turkey and Eire.

III

Having said so much about denials of religious liberty, and about the need for religious liberty, it is about time that we defined what we mean by the term. What do we mean when we call for religious liberty? Let us begin with a few fairly authoritative Protestant definitions.

In his address as president of the Federal Council of Churches in 1942, Dean Luther A. Weigle of Yale presented a detailed definition under three main heads: (a) the religious freedom of the individual; (b) the religious freedom of the church or congregation; (c) the religious freedom of citizens. Under the religious freedom of the individual he listed freedom of belief and of worship, freedom to live and act in accord with such belief and worship, freedom of religious expression, of evangelism, of religious education, of organization, freedom to withdraw and freedom to disbelieve. Under the freedom of the church or congregation he placed freedom of assembly, of organization, of self-government, of creedal formulation, freedom to determine forms of worship, to encourage members to action in accord with belief or worship, to convert, to educate, ordain and maintain an adequate ministry, to educate children and adults, to hold property and raise funds, to cooperate with other churches. The same rights, Dr. Weigle pointed out, must be accorded unbelievers or atheists.* Under reli-

* In a vigorous attack on this claim of "rights" of religious freedom for propaganda favoring atheism, Father J. Courtney Murray, S.J., in his notable article on "Freedom of Religion" (see page 149), writes: "May I, however, say that unbelief and atheism have 'rights' as against the authority of the state? Obviously, the internal forum of the atheist's conscience, however erroneous it is, enjoys immunity from intrusion or coercion by political authority; the atheist has a right privately to practice atheism (however one does that); this right, however, is based solely on the law that limits state authority to the sphere of the common good. But has the atheist the 'right' to carry his atheism into social life by propaganda, education and organized activity, in such wise that the state would have a

gious freedom for citizens he named the right to hold the state
responsible to the moral law and to dissent in the name of conscience or religious belief from acts or requirements of the
state.

The Oxford and Madras conferences both made declarations on this subject, which cover much the same ground.
Perhaps the most succinct and at the same time authoritative
statement of the Protestant position is that adopted by the Fed-

---

moral duty to refrain from all repressive measures in his regard? This
would be an intolerable position. It would amount to a denial that the
state has a moral, as well as a material, function. To assert that the state
has a moral duty to regard with equal complacence public activity in support of religion and morality and public activity toward their destruction
would be to imply that religion and morality are in no way related to the
common good of the community, and are therefore matters of indifference
to the state. But no sane person today could accept this implication. What
ethics has always taught, experience has demonstrated *ad evidentiam* — that
disbelief in God and the moral law, and the dissemination of anti-religious
and anti-moral views are the most powerful enemies of social order. They
tend to destroy the virtue of the citizenry, in which the common good of
society chiefly consists; they likewise tend to undermine even the material
and social conditions which are the support of virtue and the common good.

"It cannot be maintained, therefore, that the state, which has the duty
of protecting the order of society even in its moral aspects, would be ex-
ceeding the limits of its ethical mandate, if it were to suppress — not with
arbitrary violence, of course, but by due process of law — public propaganda
or education designed to spread disbelief in God and in the moral law. And
there is no law that could be invoked to empower the atheist with any
'rights' against this legitimate power of the state, in such wise that he
could plead injustice, if his propagandizing activities were inhibited. Surely,
he cannot allege that his 'reason and conscience' dictate this activity; the
answer is that his reason and conscience are flatly erroneous, and are therefore not a juridically valid source of rights. I might add here that, if
atheism has a valid 'right' to propaganda, the first of Dr. Weigle's 'rights
of the citizen' becomes meaningless. This is the right 'to hold the state
itself responsible to the moral law and to God.' God and the moral law certainly forbid open attack on the foundations of religion and morality. May
not the citizen, therefore, demand that the state obey this law? And may
he not further press upon the state its strict obligation, within the limits
of its authority and by appropriate juridical means, to resist public activity
in violation of this law? If these are the citizen's rights, and the state's
obligations, they may not be nullified by any fictitious 'rights' of atheism."

eral Council of Churches and the Foreign Missions Conference of North America only last year. In its key clauses it says:

The right of individuals everywhere to religious liberty shall be recognized, and, subject only to the maintenance of public order and security, shall be guaranteed against legal provisions and administrative acts which would impose political, economic or social disabilities on the ground of religion. Religious liberty shall be interpreted to include freedom to worship according to conscience and to bring up children in the faith of their parents; freedom for the individual to change his religion; freedom to preach, educate, publish, and carry on missionary activities; and freedom to organize with others, and to acquire and hold property, for these purposes.

When it comes to defining the Catholic position, the matter becomes much more complicated. One trouble here arises out of the sources consulted. Certain Catholic individuals — notably laymen like the great English historian, Lord Acton, or the contemporary English essayist, Christopher Dawson, or the Italian liberal, Don Luigi Sturzo, or the French philosopher just appointed ambassador to the Vatican, Jacques Maritain — have given expression to views in this field which closely approximate those held by Protestants. For example, Maritain says in his book, *The Rights of Man and Natural Law:*

The first of these rights is that of the human person to make its way toward its eternal destiny along the path which its conscience has recognized as the path indicated by God. With respect to God and the truth, one has not the right to choose according to his own whim any path whatsoever; he must choose the true path, in so far as it is in his power to know it. But with respect to the state, to the temporal community and the temporal power, he is free to choose his religious path at his own risk; his freedom of conscience is a natural, inviolable right. . . . This is how we must understand the right which President Roosevelt describes as the "freedom of every person to worship God in his own way everywhere in the world."

And again, to quote further from the same book:

A vitally and truly Christian political society would be Christian by virtue of the very spirit that animates it and that gives shape to its structures, which means that it would be evangelically Christian. And because the immediate object of the temporal community is human life with natural activities and virtues, and the human common good, not divine life and the mysteries of grace, such a political society would not require of its members a common religious creed and would not place in a position of inferiority or political disadvantage those who are strangers to the faith that animates it. And all alike, Catholics and non-Catholics, Christians and non-Christians, from the moment they recognize, each in his own way, the human values of which the gospel has made us aware, the dignity and the rights of the person, the character of moral obligation inherent in authority, the law of brotherly love and the sanctity of natural law — would by the same token be drawn into the dynamism of such a society and would be able to cooperate for its common good. . . .

Obviously, indeed, for any given people, such public expression of common faith would by preference assume the forms of that Christian confession to which the history and the traditions of this people are most vitally linked. But other religious confessions could also take part in this public expression, and they would also be represented in the councils of the nation, in order that they may defend their own rights and liberties and help in the common task. . . . As for those who do not believe in God or who do not profess Christianity, if they do, however, believe in the dignity of the human person, in justice, in liberty, in neighborly love, they also can cooperate in the realization of such a conception of society, and cooperate in the common good.

Protestants would have little difficulty in reaching a working agreement with Roman Catholics for common action in defense of religious liberty if they could regard Maritain as an authoritative expositor of the Catholic position. The difficulty is that official Catholic dogma and doctrinal writing is so far at variance from the views of Maritain and other Catholic lay writers. Not to quote from this official material at tiresome length (it is almost endless in quantity), let me refer to only two sources — one the standard textbook on political practice in American Catholic colleges, and the other one of the basic encyclicals of the modern papacy.

In the textbook by the late Monsignor John A. Ryan and Father Francis J. Boland, *Catholic Principles of Politics,* which is a revision of the earlier *The State and the Church* by Dr. Ryan and Father M. F. X. Millar, the Catholic position is thus presented:

> If there is only one true religion, and if its possession is the most important good in life for states as well as individuals, then the public profession, protection and promotion of this religion and the legal prohibition of all direct assaults upon it, becomes one of the most obvious and fundamental duties of the state. For it is the business of the state to safeguard and promote human welfare in all departments of life.

It might be argued that in an overwhelmingly Protestant state this would involve legal disabilities on Catholicism; to which Dr. Ryan and Father Boland reply:

> To the objection that the foregoing argument can be turned against Catholics by a non-Catholic state, there are two replies. First, if such a state should prohibit Catholic worship or preaching on the plea that it was wrong and injurious to the community, the assumption would be false; therefore, the two cases are not parallel. Second, a Protestant state could not legally take such an attitude (although many of them did so in former centuries) because no Protestant sect claims to be infallible. Besides, the Protestant principle of private judgment logically implies that Catholics may be right in their religious convictions, and that they have a right to hold and preach them without molestation.

This Catholic textbook then argues for tolerance, but only on the ground of expediency because of the actual political situation now existing in most states, where intolerance would produce public disorder, and continues:

But constitutions can be changed, and non-Catholic sects may decline to such a point that the political proscription of them may become feasible and expedient. What protection would they then have against a Catholic state? The latter could legally tolerate only such religious activities as were confined to the members of the dissenting group. It could not permit them to carry on general propaganda nor accord their organization certain privileges that had formerly been extended to all religious corporations, for example, exemption from taxation. While all this is very true in logic and in theory, the event of its practical realization in any state or country is so remote in time and in probability that no practical man will let it disturb his equanimity or affect his attitude towards those who differ from him in religious faith.

What this amounts to, it would seem, is a plea by Father Ryan to Protestants not to worry about the Catholic theory of religious liberty and tolerance until a point has been reached at which, by virtue of the preponderance of Catholics in the population, it has become too late for Protestants to worry! As for the basis of this Catholic theory, one has but to read modern papal encyclicals. Take, for illustration, this from Leo XIII's *Libertas Humana*, issued in 1888:

. . . some things have been revealed by God: that the only-begotten Son of God was made flesh, to bear witness to the truth; that a perfect society was founded by Him — namely, the church, of which He is the head, and with which he has promised to abide to the end of the world. To this society He entrusted all the truths which He had taught, in order that it might keep and guard them and with lawful authority explain them; and at the same time He commanded all nations to hear the voice of the church, as if it were His own, threatening those who would not hear it with everlasting perdition. . . . In faith and in teaching of morality God himself made the church a partaker of his divine authority, and through his heavenly gift she cannot be deceived. She is therefore the greatest and most reliable teacher of mankind, and in her dwells an inviolable right to teach them. . . . Therefore there is no reason why genuine liberty should grow indignant, or true science feel aggrieved, at having to bear the just and necessary restraint of laws by which, in the judgment of the church and of reason itself, human teaching has to be controlled.

Reduced to its essentials, the issue here is profound and clearcut, and does not yield to any admonitions to tolerance, whether on grounds of expediency or of social philosophy. It grows out of the simple fact that Protestants and Roman Catholics are seeking two different things. When Catholics talk about religious liberty they have in mind liberty for the church. When Protestants talk about religious liberty they have in mind liberty for the individual conscience. The issue is almost as simple as that.

The Roman Catholic is not concerned with liberty for the individual conscience. He rejects that as leading to what he insists is the doctrinal anarchy of Protestantism. What he wants is liberty for the church. Recently a Jesuit theological professor, Father J. Courtney Murray, contributed to a Catholic theological quarterly * a discussion of " Freedom of Religion " so irenic in spirit, so informed on the Protestant position and withal so pungent in its examination of certain often unexamined premises in the thinking of representative Protestants, that it has had wide and serious attention among Protestants. But candor compelled Father Murray to claim:

The liberties of the church are not an aspect of political liberty, but *sui generis*. They are not simply the liberties of a voluntary association, the projection of the natural or legal rights of its in-

* *Theological Studies* (New York: America Press), Vol. VI, No. 1, March 1945.

dividual members. Rather, they are the liberties of a society that is itself juridically perfect, independent in its own sphere (spiritual, not political), and dowered with rights from another source (positive divine law) than that which is the first source of political liberties (the law of nature).

When the Roman Catholic is logically pressed he is finally forced to admit that, since there is only one true church (according to his view), and since error cannot have the same rights as truth, there is only one church whose liberty must be secured. Father Murray, in the article already referred to, is honest enough to admit that this is the true issue at the root of the tension over Evangelical mission work in Latin America. The right to proselytize, he writes,

cannot be finally settled on the political grounds of public policy, or even those of the " rights of man." Fundamentally, it is a theological question, and it takes us right back to the initial position that religious liberty (meaning here the right to make converts) is basically a problem of the church. . . . In the present economy, the obligation to " make disciples of all men " has been laid upon the church of Christ, to which his saving mission has been committed. There is, therefore, no right to make converts save in relation to one's share in this obligation. Up to this point, I dare say all professing Christians would agree. They differ always on the ultimate question, What is the church of Christ? This is the theological issue involved in the problem of missions; it lies on a deeper level than that of the relationship between religion and culture.

Indeed it does! It lies on the level of Protestantism's right to exist! But this is not the place to argue that question. All I am interested in now is showing that for the Catholic Church the problem of religious liberty simply concerns the freedom *of the church* to control its own life and the thinking of its own members. So long as that is not interfered with, Catholicism is content.

But that is not what Protestantism seeks at all.   Perhaps the goal of the religious liberty sought by Protestants has never been better expressed than in that Virginia Act for Establishing Religious Freedom, written by Thomas Jefferson:

Well aware that Almighty God hath created the mind free,

that all attempts to influence it by temporal punishments, or burthens, or by civil incapacitations, tend only to beget habits of hypocrisy and meanness, and are a departure from the plan of the holy author of our religion, who . . . chose not to propagate it by coercions . . . as was in his Almighty power to do,

that the impious presumption of legislators and rulers, civil as well as ecclesiastical, who, being themselves but fallible and uninspired men, have assumed dominion over the faith of others . . . hath established and maintained false religions over the greatest part of the world and through all time:

that to compel a man to furnish contributions of money for the propagation of opinions which he disbelieves, is sinful and tyrannical . . .

that our civil rights have no dependence on our religious opinions, any more than our opinions in physics or geometry;

and therefore the proscribing any citizen as unworthy [of] the public confidence by laying upon him an incapacity of being called to offices of trust and emolument, unless he profess or renounce this or that religious opinion, is depriving him injudiciously of those privileges and advantages to which . . . he has a natural right;

that it tends also to corrupt the principles of that very religion it is meant to encourage by bribing, with a monoploy of worldly honors and emoluments, those who will externally profess and conform to it . . .

that to suffer the civil magistrate to intrude his powers into the field of opinion . . . is a dangerous fallacy, which at once destroys all religious liberty . . .

that it is time enough for the rightful purposes of civil government for its officers to interfere when principles break out into overt acts against peace and good order;

and finally, that truth is great and will prevail if left to herself;

that she is the proper and sufficient antagonist to error, and has nothing to fear from the conflict, unless by human interposition disarmed of her natural weapons, free argument and debate;

errors ceasing to be dangerous when it is permitted freely to contradict them:

We the General Assembly of Virginia do enact that no man shall be compelled to frequent or support any religious worship, place, or ministry whatsoever, nor shall be enforced, restrained, molested, or burthened in his body or goods, or shall otherwise suffer, on account of his religious opinions or belief; but that all men shall be free to profess, and by argument to maintain, their opinions in matters of religion, and that the same shall in no wise diminish, enlarge, or affect their civil capacities.

Study those words, holding them against the background of the time in which they were written, and you will come to understand why the man who wrote them asked that his tombstone should say nothing of the civil honors with which his life was filled but should speak of him only as " author of the Declaration of Independence, of the Statute of Virginia for Religious Freedom, and Father of the University of Virginia."

IV

There is today widespread agitation in favor of the formulation of what has come to be popularly known as a World Bill of Rights. Some would have had such a charter of liberties written into the Charter of the United Nations Organization when that body was formed at San Francisco. That it was not done was largely on account of the difficulty of reaching agreement with the Soviet Union as to the meaning of guarantees of freedom of speech, of the press, of assembly, of religion and so on. Undiscouraged by the difficulties encountered at San Francisco, there are many who hope that such a document may soon be worked out and adopted as a supplement to the

Charter (after all, is not the American Bill of Rights an amendment?) so that it may become a test of fitness for the admission of now debarred states to the world body. In any case, the proposal is one of the utmost importance, and those who are concerned for the protection and spread of religious liberty may well give it their utmost support.

However, for the furtherance of this movement there are certain things needed. First of all, there is need for far more study in Protestant circles of the whole problem of religious liberty, of the present status of religious liberty throughout the earth, and of the hindrances which stand in the way of the enjoyment of such liberty by the majority of living men. If we do this we will come to see that religious liberty is but one of the civil liberties to which all free men have a right, and that the obtaining of religious liberty will accompany naturally and inevitably the obtaining of the other liberties — of speech, of assembly, of organization, of publication, and all the others in a true Bill of Rights — and cannot exist except precariously and in monopolistic fashion where these other liberties are not recognized. We will also come to see that all forms of state totalitarianism and tyranny are by their nature inimical to the enjoyment of any religious liberty.

Second, if we thus promote a wider and more thorough study of this issue, we will presently discover that we are a long way yet from reaching agreement, even within the Christian community, as to what it really is that we want when we demand religious freedom. Might not this wisely be one of the early tasks of the World Council of Churches — to foster a series of discussions with the proper authorities of the Roman Catholic communion, with the various branches of the Orthodox faith and with the churches in Protestant countries where an establishment of religion by the state persists, to see whether some common ground of agreement, or at the very least some *modus operandi*, might be arrived at under which the fullest measure of equality before the law, autonomy in the conduct of the churches, and freedom of the believer or non-believer to worship and practice the teachings of his religion or to refuse to worship, might be attained?

But if we do these things, let us make it perfectly clear that we do them in no spirit of apology for the Protestant position. The Protestant heritage of religious liberty, so well summarized in that statement by the Federal Council and the Foreign Missions Conference which was quoted earlier, is one of the principal glories of the Protestant tradition. We should not, for the sake of easier relations either with the state or with the authoritarian branches of Christendom, for one moment give the impression that we might under any circumstances be induced to give up any of these claims to liberty. It is an essential element of human freedom which is at stake here. The liberty of the church — that must be maintained at any cost. Yes, but equally we must show our determination to maintain that which Luther called the *Liberty of a Christian Man*. For until the freedom of man to worship in accord with the dictates of conscience is assured, the spiritual vitality of the churches in which man worships remains in peril. And where the spiritual vitality of the churches is low, the temptation to the state to reach toward totalitarian controls becomes well-nigh irresistible.

CHAPTER VII

MORAL LAW AND THE LIFE OF NATIONS

The fundamental criticism of the totalitarian state made by the Christian church is directed against its claim to moral authority. It is the perversion of ethical values which declares that " the good is that which is good for the state," which brings all religion in the Judeo-Christian tradition into antagonism with all such modern conceptions of the state. And of course it is this very attempt to identify the interests of the state with the good, the right, the true, it is this effort to make ethical values a by-product of state policies, which constitutes in the eyes of the churches the blasphemy of Leviathan. It is at this point that the state, reaching after all power, finally makes the claim which justifies Hobbes in calling it a " mortal god." To acknowledge such claims can only be, in the Christian view, idolatry.

Over against this claim on the part of the modern state to define the good and right in terms of its own interests, the churches set the conception of the authority of the moral law. It is seldom indeed nowadays that a Christian or Jewish declaration bearing on political or social issues fails to claim as its justification for speaking the authority of the moral law. This, for example, is the point of departure from which Pope Pius XII addressed his many admonitions to rulers and nations engaged in prosecuting the recent war. By way of illustration, let me quote briefly from only three.

Almost immediately after the outbreak of the war, in October 1939, the pope issued his encyclical *Summi Pontificatus* in which he said:

It is indispensable for the existence of harmonious and lasting contacts and of fruitful relations, that the peoples recognize and observe those principles of international natural law which regulate their normal development and activity. . . . To tear the law of nations from its anchor in divine law, to base it on the autonomous will of states, is to dethrone that very law and deprive it of its noblest and strongest qualities. . . . Once the bitterness and cruel strifes of the present have ceased, the new order of the world, of national and international life, must rest no longer on the quicksands of changeable and ephemeral standards that depend only on the selfish interests of groups and individuals. No, they must rest on the unshakable foundation, on the solid rock of natural law and divine revelation.

Two months later, in his famous Christmas allocution of 1939, when the pope first laid down his basic five points of a lasting peace, his fifth point " condemned to ultimate failure " all attempts at peace-making not based on " that spirit of intimate, acute responsibility that measures and weighs human statutes according to the holy, unshakable rules of Divine Law," and interestingly enough went on to identify the principles of the moral law with those of the Beatitudes. And in the magnificent Christmas allocution of 1941, Pius outlined in detail a whole conception of a new Europe, based on this foundation:

Such a new order, which all peoples desire to see brought into being after the trials and ruins of this war, must be founded on that immutable and unshakable rock, the moral law which the Creator Himself has manifested by means of the natural order and which He has engraved with indelible characters in the hearts of men: that moral law whose observance must be inculcated and fostered by the public opinion of all nations and of all states with such a unanimity of voice and energy that no one may dare to call into doubt or weaken its binding force.

Equally have Protestants, in their approach to these issues, based their claims to be heard on the authority of the moral law. Thus, the Study Conference on the Churches and a Just and Durable Peace held at Delaware, Ohio, in March 1942, opened its " Message " with a list of thirteen Guiding Principles, of which these were the first two:

We believe that moral law, no less than physical law, undergirds our world. There is a moral order which is fundamental and eternal, and which is relevant to the corporate life of men and the ordering of human society. If mankind is to escape chaos and recurrent war, social and political institutions must be brought into conformity with this moral order.

We believe that the sickness and suffering which afflict our present society are proof of indifference to, as well as direct violation of, the moral law. All share in responsibility for the present evils. There is none who does not need forgiveness. A mood of genuine penitence is therefore demanded of us — individuals and nations alike.

At the International Round Table of Christian Leaders held at Princeton, New Jersey, in July 1943 — a Protestant gathering of importance because it contained representatives from all parts of the British Commonwealth as well as from Holland, France, China and, unofficially, from Germany and Japan — the Delaware declaration on the authority of the moral law was reaffirmed, and these words added:

This moral order is the will of God, the Creator of mankind. Basic in it are the law of justice and the principle that man should love his neighbor as himself. The Christian church believes and declares the gospel that God in Christ enables man to overcome his sinful defiance of the moral order. While such defiance persists, those who seek to do his will must strive to restrain the power and effect of evil, and to introduce order into society by extending to human relationships the rule of just and good laws.

Finally, as an indication of the like-mindedness of all religious groups on this issue, it should be noted that when members of the Federal Council of Churches, the National Catholic Welfare Conference and the Synagogue Council of America issued the joint "Declaration on World Peace" in October 1943 which became popularly known as the "Pattern for Peace," they opened it with this affirmation: "The organization of a just peace depends upon practical recognition of the fact that not only individuals but nations, states and international society are subject to the sovereignty of God and to the moral law which comes from God."

II

It is not difficult to understand why there should be this renewed insistence on the fact and authority of the moral law (or, as Roman Catholics are more likely to call it, the natural law). The chaotic and dissolving nature of contemporary life has aroused in most of us, even the most pragmatic, a new desire for some absolutes. We want something that we can take hold of and be sure that it will not vanish in our grasp. In nothing is this more true than in the realm of morals. We trace a direct connection between the relativistic interpretation of morals which has held sway in Western education for a generation or longer and the dissolution which is overtaking family life, the hard cynicism which afflicts so much of Western society, and even the unrestrained egoism of the modern state. After all, if there are no moral absolutes, on what basis can we convict a Nazi state of wrong when it teaches the German people that whatever serves the purposes of the state is right and good? We feel the need to reach again that confident spirit in which the prophet can stand forth in the presence of all principalities and powers with his challenge, " Thus saith the Lord! "

It is in response to this sense of human need that the Chris-

tian church is insisting with a new urgency on recognition of
the moral law. It believes that among men with full faculties,
without regard to environment either of time or of culture,
there always has been, there is now, and there always will be
a sense of inner *oughtness* — closely analogous to what Kant
called a moral imperative — which has constituted a natural law
for the ordering of men's relations with their fellows — a law
not given by any state, but anterior to any state; a law written
into man's being at the moment of creation by his Creator.
Or, as the Catholic philosopher, Jacques Maritain, puts it in
his *The Rights of Man and Natural Law:*

> The idea of natural law is a heritage of Christian and classical
> thought. It does not go back to the philosophy of the eighteenth
> century, which more or less deformed it, but rather to Grotius,
> and before him to Suarez and Francisco de Vitoria; and further
> back to St. Thomas Aquinas; and still further back to St. Augus-
> tine and the church fathers and St. Paul; and even further back
> to Cicero, to the Stoics, to the great moralists of antiquity and its
> great poets, particularly Sophocles. *Antigone* is the eternal
> heroine of natural law, which the ancients called *the unwritten
> law*, and this is the name most befitting it.

To make the conception clearer it may be well to look
briefly at what the idea was which Cicero expressed, and which
makes Maritain regard him as one of the fathers of the idea of
an authoritative moral law. In his *De Legibus* this Roman of
the pre-Christian era insists

> that we are born for justice, and that right is founded not in
> opinion but in nature. There is indeed a true law (*lex*), right
> reason, agreeing with nature and diffused among all, unchanging,
> everlasting, which calls to duty by commanding, deters from
> wrong by forbidding. . . . Nor is it one law at Rome and an-
> other at Athens, one law today and another hereafter; but the
> same law, everlasting and unchangeable, will bind all nations and

all times; and there will be one common Lord and ruler of all, even God, the framer and proposer of this law.*

So this conception of an innate law, or conception of rights and responsibilities recognized by all men with full faculties, superior to all human law, has persisted down through the centuries.   It received its fullest formulation in the Scholastic philosophy of St. Thomas Aquinas, and Roman Catholic thinkers today characteristically return to St. Thomas for their governing ideas when they are discussing it.   But it is worth noting, in our own tradition of law, that such a fount as Blackstone, in the introduction to his famous *Commentaries*, held that the " law of nature being coeval with mankind and dictated by God Himself is, of course, superior in obligation to any other. It is binding all over the globe in all countries and at all times; no human laws are of any validity if contrary to this."   And Locke held essentially the same position: " The state of nature has a law of nature to govern it, which obliges every one; and reason, which is that law, teaches all mankind who will but consult it that being all equal and independent, no one ought to harm another in his life, health, liberty or possessions."   Locke also insisted that " the law of nature stands as an eternal rule to all men, legislators as well as others."

It is plain how this principle, as Locke enunciated it, influenced the thinking of the men who made the American Revolution and wrote our Declaration of Independence.   This has been effectively pointed out by the Catholic essayist, Christopher Dawson, who writes in *The Judgment of the Nations:*

. . . as Troeltsch points out, the great experiment of the Cromwellian Commonwealth, short-lived though it was, by the momentum of its religious impulse opened the way for a new type

* For an inclusive and scholarly treatment of the classical conception of moral law, see "The Law of Nature in Greco-Roman Thought," by James Luther Adams, in the *Journal of Religion*, April 1945.

of civilization based on the freedom of the person and of conscience as rights conferred absolutely by God and nature. The connection is seen most clearly in America where the Congregational Calvinism of New England which was a parallel development to the Independent Puritanism of old England, developing from the same roots in a different environment, leads on directly to the assertion of the Rights of Man in the constitutions of the North American states and to the rise of political democracy. Calvin . . . regarded the natural law in the traditional way as identical with the moral law, as the norm to which all social and individual behavior must conform and which rests, in the last resort, on the will of God, as revealed to man's reason and conscience.

It would be of interest, if space allowed, to make this historical review of the development of the idea of moral law more complete. But this will suffice to show how large a body of agreement, stretching at least as far back as Greece of the fifth century B.C. (and concurred in by the sages of the East), there is for the assertion of the existence of this moral, or natural, law, which the two eminent American Catholic authorities, Monsignor John A. Ryan and Father Francis J. Boland, in their *Catholic Principles of Politics* define as " a necessary rule of action, determined by rational nature, imposed by God as author of nature and perceived intuitively. It is a necessary rule of action because without it man would have no basic moral guide or standard and could not live a rational life."

That last statement by Fathers Ryan and Boland really sums up the reason why this concept of the authority of the moral law has become so important to the Christian churches in their dealings with the modern state. " Without it man would have no basic moral guide." In other words, in the moral law the churches believe that they have something which is in the nature of both anchor and weapon. Anchor by which to find moral stability in the midst of the contemporary chaos; weapon by which to cut one's way through the jungle of ethical relativisms in which we find ourselves. By virtue of the moral law, the churches are provided with what seems like a simple, clearcut, easily announced and easily understood approach alike to the state, to corporate groups and to individuals. " Here is the moral law. Obey it and live. Defy or disregard it and perish."

I find myself in full sympathy with this development. I agree as to the importance and authority of the moral law. I am glad to see this conception receiving the sort of attention in Protestant circles which it has long commanded in Catholic. I believe, with those who formulated the Guiding Principles of Delaware, that states which ignore or flout the demands of the moral law will indeed perish. I agree that for all of us, whether as individuals or in our corporate relationships, there is a basic *oughtness*, something about which argument is superfluous because it lies beyond the reach of choices, something that cannot be denied without moral disaster. I think there is nothing more needed in such relations as the churches have with the state than renewed emphasis on the actuality and authority of this innate law.

III

But (yes, here comes the inevitable " but ") there are limitations and cautions which need to be kept in mind when the church confronts the state in the name of the moral law, or when it confronts any of the organizations of society. The rule which the moral law provides is not quite the simple, clear-cut, open-and-shut, easily grasped imperative that it is sometimes presented as being, and that we all frequently wish it were. The applications and interpretations of the moral law are not automatic. Always they are subject to the environmental limitations of the interpreter. The law may be immutable, but its expounders are not. Reinhold Niebuhr has pointed this out with great cogency in the case of St. Thomas Aquinas. There is much in Aquinas which is of lasting value in developing the theory of the moral law and its philosophical nature. But St. Thomas as the *expositor* of moral law was simply a man of his own times, and his vast apparatus of applications therefore became simply an attempt to freeze the norms of medieval society. It is hardly too much to say that the natural law as conceived by St. Thomas in actual working was mainly a glorification of the values of feudalism.

A little reflection on the ways in which the natural, or moral, law has been appealed to in justification of all sorts of human abuses should be enough to induce extreme caution in claiming divine sanction for any specific applications which may be put forward. In the name of the moral law men have justified the political theory of despotism, the denial of women's rights, the horrors of religious persecution, and the cruelties of colonial conquest. And the more detailed the efforts to apply the moral law to the political or social problems of a period, the greater is the danger that the application will take on the environmental coloration of the interpreter. In fact, the more one reflects upon this problem of the relation of the mind of the interpreter to the interpretation, the more one is likely to move toward agreement with those who hold that the only moral law of whose existence and authority we can be sure is the law of love.

Yet if, in the final analysis, the moral law turns out to be the law of love, we are still faced with the problem of interpretation and application. And no one — not even the zealot in a carefully selected community of zealots withdrawn from practically all contact with the rest of the world — would contend that this is easy. For instance, consider the divisions among equally sincere Christians over the application of the law of love to the problem of war or to that of the treatment of enemies.

The late Archbishop of Canterbury, Dr. William Temple, was probably as searching a theological thinker, and as great-souled a Christian, as the contemporary Western church has known. Nevertheless, the record shows how he wrestled with the question as to what to do, consistent with Christian teaching, with Germany. The archbishop agreed that Christianity enjoins the forgiveness of enemies, and he would have agreed with the Delaware Conference that " it is contrary to the moral order that nations in their dealings with one another should be motivated by a spirit of revenge and retaliation." But there can be no forgiveness after the pattern of Christ on the cross, he held, without self-immolation, and no nation is capable of that. Therefore some other course of action is required — one that is at least within the possibility of being embraced by a nation, but at the same time is not out of accord with the law of love.

Faced by this dilemma the archbishop finally came to the conclusion that the infliction of a penalty on Germany for her aggression would be the utmost possible application in this case of the moral law, for that would at least involve no condoning of wrong. Before he died, however, we are told he had changed this view, in the light of the awful punishment already visited on German cities and the German people by bombers and invading armies, holding that this " constitutes a penalty for German aggression so great that no other can be called for." In a preface which he wrote for a book by Stephen Hobhouse, *Christ and Our Enemies*, the archbishop said: " Whatever may be appropriate as a policy for the checking of future aggression and the establishment of security in Europe, or as an execution of justice in relation to some individuals, any thought of ' punishing Germany ' more than the course of the war is punishing her must henceforth be excluded from the minds of those who are under obligation to find and to follow the way of Christ."

These are noble words, with which I find myself in full personal agreement. But they leave us quite in the dark as to what the position of Dr. Temple would be on the nature of a positive application of the moral law to the treatment of Germany. And there will be hosts of Christians, quite as sincere in their Christian allegiance if not as eminent, who will disagree with the archbishop's position even as a negative application of the requirements of the law of love.

As to the difficulty of application in the case of the other problem which was suggested for illustrative purposes — the relation of the law of love to the fact of war — it is sufficient simply to point to the presence in the churches of both pacifists and non-pacifists to show how far Christians are from an agreed-on interpretation.

For myself, I have found most satisfaction in trying to work out the *application* of the moral law in terms of building the sense of community among men. It seems to me that all the evidence we have — anthropological and biological as well as sociological and theological — indicates that God created us to live in communities. The goal toward which we should be striving is that of an eventual world community in which all shall dwell as brothers, sons of the one Heavenly Father, whose mind for us was revealed when our Lord taught us to pray that the Kingdom should come on earth in which the will of God should be done as it is in heaven. With that as a starting premise, it seems to me that the moral law — the law of love — may be best apprehended and applied by testing our acts, our attitudes and our intentions according to their effects on the building of this community desired by God.

When it comes to the actual problem of application, I begin with myself, for there is nowhere else to begin. And I see that if I do not commit myself to loyalty to my best insights, my noblest aspirations, I finally become unfit to live with myself, and so am worthless as a member of any wider community.

That, of course, was what Shakespeare was talking about in the familiar lines spoken by Polonius:

> To thine own self be true,
> And it must follow, as the night the day,
> Thou canst not then be false to any man.

But from that start I move outward. I must be loyal to others; otherwise I am a hypocrite and a double-dealer, and no community of hypocrites and double-dealers can hold together long. More than that, I must have an active concern for the welfare of others; otherwise in my drive to get ahead I will try to destroy them, and they, in order to protect themselves, will try to destroy me, and so again our community will be broken to bits. If I possess power or position or wealth or any other advantage, I must hold this at the service of others; it is a notable fact that this sense of the obligation of power is to be found in every culture from the moment man begins to form societies. And finally, I must have an active desire to see justice done, the balances held even, the principles of the Golden Rule put into practice; for without this sense of a principle of justice operating among men, community cannot survive. The application of the moral law, or of the law of love, thus just about reduces in practice to this — that what serves to build community I will judge to be in accord with that law, and what serves to disrupt community I will judge to be in contravention of it.

Now I believe that this attempt to apply the moral law, or to bring it within working limits, has validity. I believe that it fits as much as we know of the working of that law in all societies and among all men at all times. I believe that it supplies a comprehensible method of application for today. Nevertheless, I would not want to make too sweeping claims for it. Because it is the working basis at which I have arrived as a child of this century living in this particular kind of society, I recog-

nize that it may not seem either so convincing or so practically
helpful to those of another century or within another cultural
environment. In other words, I recognize that the relativity
which we try to get rid of when we proclaim the authority of
the moral law slips in the back door again when we turn to the
task of applying it.

IV

Nor does this fully explore the difficulties which are involved in proclaiming the moral law as the guide in the life
of nations. For the assertion of the authority of the moral
law usually carries with it the assumption that men and nations can keep that law. But can they? Is this not rather the
very dilemma which St. Paul asserts lies at the core of all
human aspirations after the good life:

> . . . for to will is present with me; but how to perform that
> which is good I find not.
> For the good that I would, I do not: but the evil which I would
> not, that I do.
> Now if I do that I would not, it is no more I that do it, but sin
> that dwelleth in me.
> I find then a law, that, when I would do good, evil is present
> with me.
> For I delight in the law of God after the inward man:
> But I see another law in my members, warring against the law
> of my mind, and bringing me into captivity to the law of sin
> which is in my members.
> O wretched man that I am! who shall deliver me from the body
> of this death?
>
> (Romans 7:18–24)

" To will is present with me; but how to perform that which
is good I find not." There speaks the voice of human experience, a product of the centuries. But this failure of the will to
do that which reason and instinct (if there is any such thing)

and even enlightened self-interest enjoin, remains a baffling and unsolved problem — unsolved, that is, for us as individuals except in terms of the grace of God on whom St. Paul casts himself in his despair when he cries, " Who shall deliver me? I thank God through Jesus Christ our Lord! "

Yet we are trying to deal here with the infinitely more difficult problem of the moral responsibility of the *state*. The state says, " What I will is for you the basic good. Do that, and you shall prosper." We reject this. In fact, we turn the tables on the state and say, " Obey the moral law and live; disobey it and die." But *can* the state obey the moral law? Has it the resources of understanding and unselfishness and, more than all else, of *will* to obey? It is now a good many years since Reinhold Niebuhr wrote his *Moral Man and Immoral Society*. I understand that he has said that if he were writing it today there are a good many revisions he would make in the argument of that book. However, I regard it as still the most searching, or at least the most thought-provoking, volume he has written, and it seems to me that the thesis he so memorably summarized in that title is profoundly and dismayingly true. Man as an individual *is* a far more accountable moral being than man merged in a group. Many a man has done things as an indistinguishable unit in a lynching mob that are wholly incomprehensible and revolting to him when he wakes up alone with a hangover on the morning after. And the lynching need not be a physical one; college professors and doctors of divinity have character- and career-lynching bees of their own.

Our social contrivances continue to grow increasingly impersonal, and as they grow impersonal they grow irresponsible. " We are a nation with the duty to survive," said the Supreme Court in the Macintosh case, and there are plenty of political philosophers who will argue that the state cannot, because of its nature, admit any higher, or indeed any other, moral duty than the duty to survive. Those treasurers of church benevolent boards who were mentioned in an earlier chapter had no desire to evade their moral obligations; they simply did not agree that they had any moral obligation, in the case of such impersonal social agencies, beyond the obligation to survive — or in other words, to see that they got the highest rate of interest consonant with safety on the investments for which they were responsible.

Now, how far *are* the processes of government amenable to the dictates of the moral law? If we define that law as the law of love, the answer becomes anything but easy. Could a state survive that consistently attempted to live up to the Sermon on the Mount, which is probably as distinguished an exposition of the law of love as we have? It may be argued that it could. It may be argued that it cannot survive permanently on any other basis. But one thing cannot be argued — it cannot be argued that there is any state in the world today that is willing to trust its existence to the experiment. Least of all, I suspect, the United States.

The reality of this problem is historically demonstrated by the number of times communal groups, seeking to apply the moral law as they interpreted it in their relations with government, have ended by virtually withdrawing from the world, either migrating to some empty spot of earth or making an agreement in which, by withdrawing from all civic participation, they have sought to wash their hands of any complicity in the acts of the state or moral responsibility therefor. Moreover, the record of rulers who claimed to follow the highest moral lights is not such as will furnish us much reassurance. Recall only a few comparatively recent instances.

William Penn, as the benevolent proprietor of Pennsylvania and a convinced Quaker, probably came as near to obeying the moral law in his conduct of affairs of state as any other ruler in modern history. Yet in Macaulay's *History of Eng-*

land there is scarcely any character who is presented as more of a hypocrite, a time-server, a fawning intriguer in behalf of reaction and tyranny. To be sure, Macaulay is not an unbiased witness. He is capable of cruel injustices and he is always susceptible to the journalist's temptation to paint his scenes in violent colors. That he surely did in this instance. But the point is that there were enough episodes even in the career of William Penn to make possible with only a modicum of distortion such a distressing picture as Macaulay has left us.

Or consider Gladstone. I presume there have been few modern statesmen who have tried more faithfully (at least in their own estimation) to conduct their ministry of state on the highest level of moral responsibility. Yet there have been few more widely accused by their contemporaries of hypocrisy and moral deceit. One recalls Disraeli's scathing comment, that he did not mind Gladstone's playing politics with an ace always tucked up his sleeve, but he did object to his claiming that it had been God who had put it there!

Think of Alexander I and his Holy Alliance, whose charter opened with the declaration:

> In the name of the Most Holy and Indivisible Trinity . . . Their Majesties the Emperor of Austria, the King of Prussia, and the Emperor of Russia, having . . . acquired the intimate conviction of the necessity of settling the steps to be observed by the Powers, in their reciprocal relations, upon the sublime truths which the Holy Religion of Our Saviour teaches: They solemnly declare that the present Act has no other object than to publish, in the face of the whole world, their fixed resolution, both in the administration of their respective States, and in their political relations with every other government, to take for their sole guide the precepts of that Holy Religion, namely, the precepts of Justice, Christian Charity, and Peace.

Well, we all remember where the Holy Alliance ended, and where Alexander I ended. If the conference at Potsdam had come forth with a declaration that henceforth Harry S. Truman, Clement Attlee, and Josef Stalin meant to take for their sole guide the precepts of justice, Christian charity and peace, most of us would have felt that there was more reason than ever to be apprehensive as to the fate of the postwar world.

Or think of the two most recent rulers who professed to conduct their states according to religious principles. Both of them, I believe, were quite honest in their claims to be ruling with the highest sense of moral responsibility. I have in mind Paul Kruger in the Boer Republic and the ill-fated Engelbert Dollfuss in Austria. Kruger almost literally ruled with a Bible in his hand, and Dollfuss constantly sought and followed the admonitions of the Roman Catholic Church. Nevertheless, the policies which Kruger backed for the subjugation and terrorizing of the blacks in the Transvaal must fill any humanitarian soul with horror, while Dollfuss' Christian state wound up blasting the families of Socialist workers out of the model municipal apartment houses in Vienna with artillery fire, and destroying the most honest and humanitarian municipal government anywhere in Europe outside Scandinavia.

Is it possible for the state to obey the moral law? The art of politics, John Morley insisted, is the art of compromise — and Morley was about as uncompromising an idealist in politics as our times have known; so much so that in 1914 he resigned from the British cabinet rather than sanction his country's participation in the First World War. But how can compromise and the conception of an eternal, unchanging and always authoritative moral law go together? Some modern churchmen, who are so enamored of the dialectical approach that they apparently feel that when they have announced a paradox they have discharged their duty as moral guides, are content to bring the issue now under consideration up to this paradox and leave it here. Is there not, however, something more that can be said — something besides admonitions to rely on the grace of God — something that will bear upon the inescapable fact that after all states, like individuals, have to go on functioning?

I believe that there is. I believe that we can approach this problem — the problem of the observance of the moral law by the state — much as we approach that other problem — the problem of attaining justice in the actions of the state. As a matter of fact, of course, these are but two aspects, two faces of the same problem. Can the state do justice? No more than the individual — not if what you mean is perfect justice, justice fully and eternally in accord with the will of God. There is no such thing as perfect justice among men, and we do not seriously object when it is said that there never will be. But we have found that despair over attaining perfection in this regard need not inhibit action pointed toward high goals. St. Thomas Aquinas has been a help to Christian thought at this point with his conception of " rough justice " — the justice that takes the frailties of human understanding and will into account, yet is constantly lifting the conduct of men and societies toward higher levels.

Now it seems to me that here likewise we have to acknowledge our inability to attain perfection in the application of the moral law. We never have; we never will. But what we can hope for is action, by the individual and even by the state, *in the direction* of the ends which the moral law has in view. We can at least labor to secure a much more serious effort to approximate the requirements of the moral law in social as well as in individual action than has hitherto been known. We can labor likewise to strip away from our social personalities — our corporations, our communities, our states — that protective outer covering of anonymous irresponsibility which they are continually casting about themselves. At the very least, we of the churches can throw our strength into the effort to insure that our states no longer profess to act in ignorance of the moral law, and still less in defiance of it. And we can cultivate that sensitivity to truth by which we can keep our own selves and the community and the state aware of the gap which still yawns between the performance and that requirement of the moral law which is the perfect will of God. Then, and only then, in the words of the apostle, " having done all," we may stand — and leave the rest to the grace of God.

v

What, then, can be said as to the prospect of restraining Leviathan by demanding that the state subject itself to the requirements of the moral law? In order to summarize as briefly as possible, let me present six conclusions at which, in my own thinking regarding this question, I have arrived.

First, it seems to me that the churches should welcome the reassertion of the reality and authority of the moral law which is going on so widely. They should not only welcome it; they should see in it their only firm basis for dealing with governments and other great social entities, and they should accordingly proclaim this unceasingly as their word of guidance and judgment. It will take generations of unremitting prophetic preaching before our states will believe that " social and political institutions must be brought into conformity with the moral order," but this must be done if our domestic society is not to be a battlefield and if our world is not to be drowned in blood every generation.

Second, the churches, while proclaiming the reality and authority of the moral law, must recognize the difficulties which still inhere in the attempt to define it and, even more, to apply it. The work of the great minds of the past in this field is not all lost. For example, I believe that any Protestant is bound to be both stimulated and enlightened by the treatment given the question of the natural law in the writings of St. Thomas Aquinas. But the subject is by no means as crystal clear as

Catholic theologians would have one believe, or as some Protestant leaders, in their joy at finding an alternative to the popular moral relativism of recent years, now inferentially hold.
There are vast aspects of this subject which still need to be
explored, only a few of which I have been able to indicate in
this discussion. The churches, therefore, should return to the
study of the idea of the moral law, and its applicability in the
contemporary world, with a resoluteness which Protestantism,
at least, has not displayed since the Reformation.

Third, I am convinced that the churches will find their
most fruitful method of attempting to apply the moral law to
the conditions of modern life if, as I have said, they interpret
it as a means of building community. That, when all is said
and done, has become the supreme problem for modern man
and for the modern state. How can the anarchic tendencies
which are reducing our existence on this planet to a shambles
be checked? How can we build firm and enduring communities, which shall ever enlarge their boundaries until that day
when we have a world community which is more than a name
but is rather the blessed experience of every living person?
Those are the great questions which confront states as well
as men. The moral law, interpreted in the sense of being a
great agency for the building of community, can be so defined
and so applied as to be made to seem as important to the legis-
lator, to the corporation president, to the diplomat, to the labor
union officer as to the theologian. It can, I believe, even be so
simplified in its presentation as not to do violence to its truth
and yet to make it easily grasped, in its essentials, and believed
by people in the mass. "Does this act, this law, this policy
help to build community? Then it is in accord with the moral
law. Does it destroy the basis or the hope of community?
Then it is not in accord with the moral law." It is always the
desire of a journalist to discover an interpretation of abstract
ideas which the person with only rudimentary intelligence

can seize hold on and act by. Such, I believe, is this interpretation of the moral order as an order of community, and the moral law as the agency by which community is being built and is to be built.

Fourth, in presenting the claims of the moral law the churches should beware the pitfall of utopianism. If, in the last analysis, the moral law is the will of God, we know that finite man can never apprehend the full will of God, much less do it. Now there is a real peril, if the moral law is presented as an inflexible standard which must be fully attained in order to escape catastrophe, that in men's perception of the relative nature of their moral achievements they may lose heart. It remains true that when we have done the best we can, in the light of God's righteousness we have still to say that we are unprofitable servants. Nevertheless, we can escape this peril of utopianism if, instead of emphasizing the extent of our shortcomings, we take every occasion to press the struggle for moral achievement and to thank God for whatever small measure of attainment is won. The state, as well as the individual, that is admonished to obey the moral law must be given a sense of *possibility*, even though we may know that this is limited possibility. Otherwise, the admonition will fall on deaf ears.

Fifth, and the other side of the consideration just presented, the churches in advancing the claims of the moral law should beware lest they betray a readiness to accept less than the utmost in possible moral achievement. The very fact that there is peril of a utopianism which would cut the nerve of action helps to create a peril of compromise. Men, both as individuals and in the group, are capable of greater moral achievements than they are frequently given credit for being able to compass. Here, if I may venture to pass a judgment, is the point at which the Roman Catholic Church, despite the firmness of its insistence on the demands of the moral law during generations when Protestantism has said all too little about it, has frequently gone astray in its attempts to guide its sons in the application of that law. Realizing the necessity for actually working in terms of approximations, and the pedagogical value of not setting the sights too high, this great church has on many occasions set the sights too low. The individual and society will always set the sights low if their moral guides will permit it. It is the business of the churches to see that, in presenting the demands of the moral law, there is never left among men the suspicion that these can be fulfilled by immoral but simply self-regarding men and societies.

And finally, in its presentation of the claims of the moral law the church must stand by its conception of the moral order of the universe, which involves that our human failures to discharge our full obligations under the moral law — " the high that proved too high, the heroic for earth too hard," as Browning put it — even though these are implicit in our humanity, yet bring retribution. Here will always be a safe-guard against that pride and self-righteousness concerning which we are so earnestly being warned these days. Here is the point at which, at the last, the moral law will reach its limitations and the grace of God must step in and take over. The moral law of the universe is a rock on which we can destroy ourselves. The present probability is that we shall do so. We must live, therefore, in fear and trembling, trusting only that there will be enough of the grace of God to save us from the results of our folly.

CHAPTER VIII

THE CHURCH AND PRESSURE POLITICS

I

The other side of the issue discussed in the preceding chapter is the question of the extent to which the church should participate in politics. If the church declares that there is a moral law which the state must obey or perish, if the church contends that it knows the nature and requirements of this moral law, is not the church then under ethical obligation so to exert its influence in political affairs as to insure that the state will act in accord with the moral law? And does not this imply, in terms of church action in a democratic state, that the most direct, effective, open and honorable way by which the church may influence the state is through organization of its forces to act as a pressure group, a terror to wrong-doers and a strong support to those who would serve righteousness?

These, it seems to me, are questions which have to be frankly faced as soon as the church approaches the field of political action. To them, in the light of recent developments, it may now be necessary to add another. If the modern state tends to gather to itself constantly increasing resources of power, and if this concentration of power tends to create a Leviathan that is beyond moral control, is it not the part of wisdom for the church to make such political arrangements as are required to seize or guide the machinery of the state, so that (1) state power shall not be used for unworthy ends, and (2) state power shall not threaten the position or program of the church? The official encouragement of Catholic Action in many countries apparently constitutes an affirmative papal answer to this question. Should not a Protestantism aware of the dangers inherent in the trend toward state totalitarianism be making the same affirmative answer?

I am aware that, although I have tried to present these issues in as realistic and impartial a manner as possible, an undertone of rejection can be sensed beneath these questions as I have asked them. The tradition of separation of church and state is so strong in this country that I doubt whether it is possible to frame the issues for Americans in a way that does not imply an expected negative. Nevertheless, there are hosts of American churchmen, both Protestant and Catholic, who are ready to countenance, and on occasion counsel, direct intervention by the churches in political life. Not by the churches acting as such in political organization, but by the churches acting through organizations which they have been instrumental in forming, which they largely finance and keep in operation, whose policies are largely controlled by the churches which have nurtured them.

For it needs to be recognized that, paralleling the American tradition of separation of church and state, there is an equally strong tradition of political activity on the part of our American churches. The " political parson " has been a familiar figure on the national landscape from the days of our Revolution straight down to our present " Religious Associates " of the Political Action Committee of the C.I.O. It would be impossible to determine whether more Catholic priests than Protestant parsons have indulged in that soul-satisfying pastime of instructing their congregations how to vote; there have been plenty of instances in both camps. Demands by infuriated laity or politicians or newspapers that the clergy shall abstain from political activity generally mean no more than that the parsons are " interfering " on the opposite side. When the pulpit supports the political party or policy or candidate that the layman approves, then criticism turns to praise, and the parson finds himself held up as a model of courageous citizenship and a prophet of righteousness. It all depends, as someone first observed a long time ago, on whose ox is gored.

This tradition of direct church concern for the nature of politics, as well as for the total character of civilization, is of too long standing to be mistaken. Many European commentators have settled on this as the major characteristic of American church life. Almost scornfully, especially in the days before the war, they have classified the American churches as " activist." The implication has been that contemplation and devotion, scholarship and the life of the Spirit have suffered in American church life from a restless zeal to crusade, to reform, to make the will of the churches the patterns of society. American churchmen have retaliated by accusing their European brethren of " quietism." Their implication has been that European churchmanship has been so lost in introspection, mysticism, the life of personal piety that it has remained aloof from, if not indifferent to, society's plunge to destruction.

It may be that the experiences of the war years will set in motion a process of rapprochement between these European and American concepts. Each has something to teach the other. Yet it would, I am sure, be untrue to assert that the American churches, outside a few small sects, are likely in any conceivable future to move very far toward Europe's prewar pietism. On the contrary, the American churches are convinced that many of the most tragic aspects of Europe's recent social and political history trace directly back to the virtual abandonment by large portions of European Protestantism of any sense of social and political responsibility. And if reports of postwar church gatherings in Europe — especially in Germany — are to be believed, this diagnosis is now being accepted by many European Christians, who are insisting that from now on Protestantism must concern itself directly and unceasingly with the character of European political life. The trend, in other words, is such that if there is to be any fusing of European and American tendencies, the point of meeting will be well over toward what has been the American position.

The prospect, I take it, is for more rather than less " activism " in the church. Every terrified shout that, in the atomic age, the very survival of the race depends on making men spiritually fit to handle these new powers, in its way is an appeal for such " activism." The Illinois editor who, after the atomic bombs fell, wrote (in the *Pekin Daily Times*) that because our heads have developed too far beyond our hearts, he would favor having the government reduce all public school teachers' salaries to $500 a year and public school classes to one hour a week, while it paid all ministers $20,000 a year and all Sunday school superintendents $10,000 and forced all citizens to attend church schools five days a week, was simply giving exaggerated expression to the desire that thousands have felt for more rather than less " interference " by the churches in public affairs. The church which believes that it knows what kind of domestic order will bring a maximum of personal satisfactions and security, or what kind of international order will bring a maximum of peace, can hardly be expected to remain either quiet or quiescent when governmental policies are projected which would destroy its hopes both at home and abroad.

It will not remain quiescent. But will it plunge into direct political action? Will it become another political pressure group? Is that the only way by which the church can act effectively in the face of the pretensions and follies of the modern state? In seeking an answer to these questions, let us consider certain other elements in the problem.

II

One fact which the churchman needs always to bear in mind, especially when tempted to seek the solution of political problems by direct church political action, is the limitations which beset his insights and methods. Any claim by the churches to be acting in accord with the moral law — which is to say, in accord with the will of God — is, as we have already seen, subject to certain sobering conditions. In the first place, there is always the possibility of imperfect perception of the will of God. Almost any Christian, unless it be an infallible pontiff, will admit this as an abstract proposition. Yet the moment the church becomes directly engaged in politics, and tries either to bend legislatures to its demands or to induce electors to vote for the candidates whom it has approved, the requirements of political success seem to force it to abandon any sense of caution or humility and to assert its certainty that it knows what God's will and the moral law require. The result is that the church soon finds itself in a false position, which is likely to become morally untenable, and from which it will ultimately be forced to retreat with great confusion and loss of moral authority.

Recall the case of prohibition. There seldom has been greater unanimity among the evangelical churches of the United States as to the will of God in the political and social sphere than in their demand for the enactment of the Eighteenth Amendment and its supporting statutes. I am not now saying that this judgment was mistaken. Indeed, by applying the tests suggested in the previous chapter, I concur in the opinion that the liquor traffic flouts the requirements of the moral law, and that it must be the will of God that its pernicious social effects shall in some fashion be done away. Looking back at the record, however, one may question whether the method which the churches took was either wise or morally impressive. And I write this as an unreconstructed prohibitionist.

What was the record? The evangelical churches formed organizations for direct political action to " dry up the nation." Into the work of these organizations they poured immense resources in personnel, money and devoted service inspired by religious zeal. They won an impressive series of political victories — so much so that by the second decade of this century it seemed politically feasible to strike for the enactment of a prohibition amendment to the federal Constitution. The amendment was adopted and with it various supporting legislation. And then, within another decade, the whole federal legal structure for wiping out the liquor traffic was itself wiped out. Why? I am aware of the argument which places the blame on a conspiracy of moneyed interests who, conniving with press and politicians, managed to wreck the whole experiment in order to lighten their taxes. Undoubtedly the activities of the various interests which found themselves threatened, or actually hit, in the pocketbook by national prohibition played an important part in repeal. But I do not believe that these alone accounted for the passage of the Twenty-first Amendment.

The factor which played a decisive part in that reversal of public policy was the rejection by the American people of the moral pretensions on which the churches based their championing of the prohibition cause. And that rejection took place because the prohibition organizations, in their zeal to see enacted and enforced legislation which they believed to be an unquestionable moral good, resorted to methods that were morally questionable. The very term, " political dry," became a stench in the land. Yet so concentrated had become the attention of the evangelical churches on the evils of the commercialized liquor traffic that they were willing, through their political agencies, to be indifferent to anything else in a politician's record or platform, provided that he could be counted on to vote " right " on this single issue.   The result presently was that the " church forces " were disclosed to be supporting some of the most reactionary, ignorant and even personally disreputable political figures in the country, simply because they could be counted on for dry votes.   The whole issue thus became enveloped in a cloud of hypocrisy.   And from that point on I, for one, would insist that the moral law itself was at work to bring to ruin this great " experiment, noble in purpose," into which the churches had thrown so much of their energies.

I have cited this unhappy experience with the Eighteenth Amendment as a reminder that the church, when it undertakes direct political action, must always bear in mind its imperfect perception of the moral law as a revelation of the will of God. Likewise, it needs to be on its guard because of the imperfect means by which all political action is carried out.   Again, prohibition might be used for illustrative purposes.   But this is so true of *all* political action that illustrations crowd from every quarter.   The essence of the problem here lies in the fact that, to produce any political action, and especially in a democracy, the temptation is always irresistible to magnify the benefit to be gained by worthy action to such an extent that, even if modest gains are won, the ultimate public mood is likely to be one of disillusionment.   Just about as surely as the church throws itself into any campaign for political ends, its propaganda will so oversell — to use an expressive Americanism — the merits of the policy it espouses that, when the struggle is over and not too much has been achieved thereby, the reflective mind asks whether the extravagant claims made during the campaign represented a deliberate attempt to deceive or political naïveté.   Either way, the prestige of the church suffers.   Yet the very nature of politics is such that, to induce a majority to vote for candidates or policies in whose success the churches have interested themselves, this overselling will always be resorted to. The candidate must always be proclaimed the man who will save the nation; the proposed law must always be the chosen measure by which a new heaven is to be brought on earth.

Consider, for example, the claims made for woman's suffrage before the adoption of the Nineteenth Amendment. I take it that there can be no serious denial of the case for woman's suffrage as an act of human justice. To this extent it can be held in accord with the requirements of the moral law, and the tremendous efforts in its support made by the church forces can be justified. But when woman's suffrage was in the arena of public debate, and the church forces — along with others — were lining up to write it into the federal Constitution, was the argument confined to the demands of justice? Of course not. The voters had to be *moved*. And moving the voters involved assuring them that, with woman's suffrage, politics would be cleansed, social vices banished and war driven from the face of the earth! Were the church conventions that resolved in favor of woman's suffrage, the church societies that descended on state legislatures to demand its enactment, meaning to deceive when they held forth such extravagant prospects? No, certainly not. They were simply, in the excitement of the struggle, yielding to the temptation to use imperfect means in seeking what they held to be an ideal end.

Or take the campaign for American adherence to the World Court which went on intermittently throughout the Long Armistice. Again, I am writing as one who favored such adherence and rejoiced to see the churches muster what support they could in its favor. Nevertheless, I must admit that there was seldom a time, while those campaigns for American adherence were in progress, when I was not apprehensive as to what the result would be if success crowned our efforts. The limitations on the possible contribution which the court could make to securing world peace were so severe and so obvious, and the benefits which the American people were told would accrue from adherence were made to sound so limitless, that anyone who could measure the prospects objectively must have seen great disillusionment in the distance. So, I fear, there is likely to be eventual disillusionment as to what has been gained by American adherence to the San Francisco Charter, although it must be said that in this instance the churches — perhaps learning caution — made their drive for such adherence with more reserve and with less unlimited promises of utopia than in most of their past ventures in political action.

All of which is simply to say that the Christian church, if it engages in political action, should do so with a clear apprehension that the Kingdom of God on earth is not just around the corner. Its own apprehension of the will of God is too imperfect to make it possible that it could be. And its own methods for implementing its limited perceptions of God's will in political and social measures are too imperfect in wisdom and righteousness to make utopian hopes reasonable. This should make for more charity and humility than frequently characterizes church action in public affairs. The church that wants to retain the confidence of men will be neither too sure nor too condemnatory when it invades the realm of political and social action in the name of a regnant moral law.

III

Again, I believe that the church should beware of direct political action *as a church* because of the compromises that are always involved in such action. " Politics is the art of compromise." Yes, but it is hard to reconcile the practice of a required compromise with the proclamation of an inerrant moral law. I had an experience not long ago which seemed to me to epitomize the difficulties involved at this point. I will not disclose the name of my correspondent, because my sympathies were so largely with him in what he was trying to do. But I will admit my surprise that he had apparently so largely overlooked the difficulties which his proposals involved.

My correspondent, a young minister who has rendered faithful and valuable service in one of the most underprivileged sections of Chicago, suggested that the church press should launch a campaign to form a Protestant bloc to insure the triumph of righteousness in national politics. Because of the human values involved, it seemed clear to him that the cause of righteousness and the cause of the New Deal — this was in the period when there was still a recognizable New Deal — were one. Why should the Protestant churches rest content with their Social Creed and with their resolutions against social exploitation and in behalf of a more just social order? Did not an honest devotion to the general ends thus proclaimed require that they should rally their forces for direct political action in support of the national political program which, it seemed obvious to him, was the one dedicated to such ends?

I did not, in answering, enter into any argument as to the limitations of the New Deal. But I did point out that, in the terms of actual Chicago politics, Protestant support of the party which proclaimed itself the protagonist of the New Deal would involve support of a political machine of most dubious reputation. And so not only in Chicago, but in Jersey City, in Boston, in Philadelphia, in St. Louis, in most of the large cities of the nation. Such political action as this Christian minister sought would presently find the churches working in alliance with a Frank Hague, an Ed Kelly and with the machine bourbons of the south.

But if the moral compromises that would inevitably be involved in such an alliance were regarded as too demoralizing to contemplate, there could be no escape by switching allegiance to the other party. A Protestant bloc tied up with the Republicans would find itself obliged to swallow alliances with reactionary business interests in many states which, in ultimate effect, would be no less morally disastrous than an alliance with the Democratic bosses.   And if, in despair of achieving the purposes sought by throwing the weight of the Protestant community behind either of the existing major parties, the church should decide to launch a party of its own and go it alone, it would thereby escape some of the immediate dilemmas of compromise only to run the risk of precipitating the country into the horrors of religious division — a Protestant ranged against a Catholic party.   Did my correspondent believe *that* would represent the will of God?   Would *that* represent faithfulness to the requirements of the moral law in public life?

Whether his subsequent silence meant that my correspondent had at last perceived difficulties in his proposal which he previously had overlooked, or whether it meant that he had given me up as too timorous to make the sort of crusader he was seeking, I have no means of knowing.   But when I hear advocacy of direct church intervention in what is so often and so rightly called the " rough and tumble " of political action, I find myself hoping that the advocates of such a course will bear in mind that the " tumble " is generally the fall that is involved in moral compromise.

IV

From all such considerations, it seems clear to me that the only type of political " pressure " which the Christian church can employ legitimately and successfully is moral pressure on its members, and on such other individuals as may be within the reach of its influence, to act as citizens on the highest levels of citizenship they can conceive.   This, I believe, it has an inescapable moral obligation to do.   It must hold up an ideal of citizenship which thinks in terms of the common good, and that means the common good of all mankind as well as the common good in parochial and national terms. It must so stress its conception of the moral law that the necessity of the long view and of the building of community will be established as a criterion of worthy political action. And it should, as the Malvern Conference declared, impress on the minds of its members their duty to " take the fullest possible share in public life " as legislators and public officials and on " all other bodies affecting the public welfare."

But when the church exerts pressure of this kind to induce its members to participate more generally and responsibly in political affairs, let it do so with understanding of and sympathy for the difficulties which these individuals are certain to encounter. In the hurly-burly of politics they will have to make their compromises. They will have to make the necessary adjustments between the ideal and the attainable. Their personal devotion to the ends approved by moral law will always be forced to work itself out within the limitation of available means. Therefore, let the church be not too quick to criticize them if, in their efforts to make the relativities of politics serve ideal purposes, they seem at times to stumble. The church must always, of course, hold before them the requirements of moral responsibility. But it should never fail to make clear its realization of the bewildering dilemmas which all political action involves.

The church owes this sense of understanding and restraint and confidence to such of her sons as undertake political responsibilities on the higher levels of public life. When a John Foster Dulles, for example, or a Chiang Kai-shek undertakes vast enterprises of world statesmanship in a spirit of religious devotion, they have a right to expect an understanding support from the church unless and until they clearly betray the moral insights which the church has inculcated in them. But the need is just as great on the lower levels. The individual Christian who, with an equally clear sense of moral responsibility, undertakes the duties of a sheriff, a town councilman, a state assemblyman or a supervisor of a state or county institution, is just as sure to find himself involved in the sort of practical difficulties that preclude more than relatively satisfying action as is the man in a position of world prominence. The church owes these who, at its inspiration, undertake the more prosaic tasks just as much praise for their achievements and sympathy in their difficulties as it does the others.

V

There are two other observations that need to be made whenever this matter of church relation to the processes of politics is under review. The first is the New Testament reminder that the Kingdom is not to be taken by violence. I take that to mean that, in all its approaches to matters affecting the ordering of society, the church must place its reliance on persuasion, not on coercion. Its history shows how frequently it has forgotten that. But when it has forgotten, the results have not been happy. There is a reason for this reliance on persuasion which is rooted deep in human nature. This reason is that only the persuaded become cooperative members of that enlarged and improved community of mankind that we are seeking.

And the other factor which should never be forgotten is the function which the church must perform of maintaining tension with the state for the state's own good. There come times when the greatest political contribution the church has to make is that of standing off from the state and rejecting the state's policies at whatever cost to itself. This may occur even when popular sentiment seems to be overwhelmingly behind the course which the state is following. The church then can only resort to the " pressure politics " of dissent.

That is always an uncomfortable and unpopular action, but sometimes it is the only one left to a church which would be true to its religious insights.

There is a story, twice told in almost identical language in the 22nd chapter of the First Book of Kings and in the 18th chapter of the Second Book of Chronicles, which illustrates this sort of " pressure politics " in unforgettable fashion. It is the story of the prophet Micaiah, the son of Imla, and his encounter with King Ahab on the eve of that monarch's expedition against Ramoth-gilead. Ahab had brought King Jehoshaphat of Judah to his captial of Samaria to induce him to join the expedition. Four hundred prophets had been called before the two kings to pronounce on the chances of the enterprise. They knew what Ahab wanted them to say and, being thoroughly palace-broken prophets, they said it. " Go up, for the Lord will deliver it into the hand of the king."

But the report was just a little too unanimous to convince Jehoshaphat. He persisted in asking whether this represented the whole prophetic community until Ahab finally confessed: " Well, there is one other, Micaiah the son of Imla. But I hate him, for he never prophesies good concerning me, but always evil." Then Jehoshaphat insisted on hearing from Micaiah, and we have that wonderful story of the prophet urged by the palace captain to key his words to the king's wishes, of his first ironic prophecy of quick and easy victory, of Ahab's outcry against such obvious perjury, and then that magnificent passage: " I saw all Israel scattered upon the mountains, as sheep that have no shepherd: and the Lord said, These have no master; let them return every man to his house in peace."

The outcome does not seem to have been pleasant for Micaiah. But neither was it for King Ahab. And in the long run, it probably satisfied Micaiah, for he had done his bit to preserve the integrity of Israel's prophetic tradition.

There come times like that even yet when the state proves unwilling to listen to the voice of the church. Very well, then, what is the church to do? The only thing it can do is to deliver its testimony to the requirements of the moral law as clearly and unequivocally as possible, and let the consequences look after themselves. In that sense the church must never hesitate to be a " pressure group." But it is moral pressure; not the pressure of political contrivance.

CHAPTER IX

LEVIATHAN IN THE SCHOOLS

I

Stewart Herman, when attempting to analyze the drive which gave National Socialism its power in Germany, entitled his book, *It's Your Souls We Want*. The arresting phrase, he explained, was taken from a Nazi party publication. Any modern state, reaching out toward totalitarian controls, will seek the same end. It wants nothing less than mastery over the souls of its people. It will never feel itself safe with less. Terror and repression may serve to hold down a certain minimum of dissent. But without the souls of the majority — which is to say, the assent and active cooperation of the majority — no authoritarian regime, however ruthless its police methods, can long endure. The battle between Leviathan and the church is a battle for men's souls.

One inescapable first step toward mastery over men's souls requires control of the mind. For that reason, Leviathan never fails to take over the schools. They are as necessary as the courts and the legislature; more necessary than the armed forces. The more the schools can be turned into drill-halls, with all curriculum tightly controlled from the political center, with teachers disciplined to exalt the idea of state authority and of a " patriotism " which consists in unquestioning submission to state demands, and with a pervasive secularistic outlook on the world of nature and of humanity, the more will the educational process corrupt the springs of democracy and prepare for the rise of the omnipotent state.

Democracy, in the final analysis, is a religious idea. It rests on a faith — nothing more. Its basic premise is that the nature of the world and of man is what the Judeo-Christian religion has claimed. Without this religious conception of man as a child of God, and of all men as of equal worth in the eyes of God, the democratic idea utterly breaks down. Secularism, which sees man as nothing more than a creature of earth, limited and controlled by biological and environmental factors which rigidly circumscribe the area of his possible achievements, logically has come out where all the Machiavellians do come out — in the hands of Leviathan.* Unless the religious outlook can be kept in the educational process, the very schools which have been established as the bulwark and hope of democracy may presently be discovered to be our most prolific sources of cynicism, self-regarding egotism, indifference as to morality in public affairs and the worship of state power.

This is why, for the churches, the issue of the nature of public education, and especially of the relation of religious education to the public schools, has become of such moment. The problem as it confronts the churches has two aspects. The first may be brushed aside as self-seeking, yet unfortunately it is this which is most frequently to the fore in church discussions. It may be phrased in some such fashion as this: How is the church to maintain its own membership and strength in a society whose members have been indoctrinated with a secularistic outlook on life? It is because church approaches to this subject of religion in education so often start from this concern that some first-rank educators, as well as a part of the public, tend to dismiss the whole agitation as no more than an effort on the part of the churches to employ the schools to make up for their own deficiencies. That suspicion is bound to persist as long as this aspect of the problem receives major emphasis in church discussions.

* Cf. *The Machiavellians*, by James Burnham. New York: John Day Co., 1943.

But it is the second aspect which is more important, even if church blundering tends to disguise that fact. It may be stated after this manner: How is society to keep alive its faith in the democratic order if the education of its members does not contain those religious values on which the whole democratic venture rests? Here is the vital issue. And with it we come to the true basis of the current anxiety over the relation of religious teaching to the education of our citizens, and specifically over the relation of education in religion to the public schools. No problem is being more vigorously debated in church and educational circles at present. It would be impossible to conclude any study of the threat with which a rising Leviathan confronts democracy without taking up this question.

Let me say at once that this is a question on which I find myself far from having reached what seem, even to me, to be satisfactory conclusions. Indeed, I sometimes wonder whether I have reached any conclusions at all. I know that such conclusions as are here set forth are limited in scope, tentative in form, in flux. My principal consolation when I regard the unsatisfactory nature of such a condition as this is that no one else seems to be doing much better. I have read numerous books and magazine articles bearing on this subject of the relation of religion to education in a society threatened with secularist disintegration. I have listened to a good many speeches. I have studied the Lord only knows how many resolutions. Proponents of various schemes for snatching public education from its secular orientation have labored with me, in the privacy of my office and my home, with all the zeal of a sawdust-trail evangelist. And I still do not believe that any final or fully satisfactory solution for this exceedingly involved and difficult problem has been found. My Catholic friends, and some Lutherans, will, I know, indignantly take exception to any such statement. But I do not believe that their parochial schools supply the answer. As for the rest of us Protestants, when I run into one of us who is sure that he knows exactly how to deal with this problem, my first reaction, I must confess, is to suspect that he has yet to discover what the problem, in all its complexities, actually is.

We all recognize, of course, that there are certain " given " factors in this problem as we face it in the United States which cannot be left out of account. There is the principle of separation of church and state — a principle never very clearly defined (consider the language of the First Amendment), but nonetheless an element of major importance in the national mind. Today that principle, in contrast with the state of affairs when it was first enunciated, is of even greater consequence to the church than to the state, for to it the church must look in protecting its witness against the encroachments of state power. There is the close relation between religion and democratic ideals. There is the principle of majority rule. And there is the equally important principle, especially in the presence of Leviathan tendencies, of the protection of minority rights. But when, in attempting to work out a method for conserving religious values in our educational system, one takes these four " given " elements and tries to apply them in combination to specific proposals for educational reform in such a way as to insure public assent, one quickly discovers how enormous are the difficulties involved.

To make these difficulties clear, one need only ask three questions. Can we maintain separation of church and state while providing for religious education in the public schools? Can we maintain the vigor of the churches and the Christian impress on our culture without religious education in the public schools? If the answer to the two preceding questions is " No," are we not caught in a dilemma from which there is no rational escape?

Of course, I know that many churchmen — perhaps most

churchmen — will insist that there is no dilemma because the answer to the first question is " Yes," not " No." But is it? Certainly there is nothing like a preponderance of opinion to that effect in the American public mind today. In my own case, I must admit, the whole issue would clear up astonishingly, and I am sure I could press forward at once to clear and final conclusions, if I could only persuade myself that the answer to that first question is certainly in the affirmative. There are times when I can — almost. But never conclusively.

I regard the methods through which churchmen have tried to escape from this dilemma (or deny its existence) by working out some plan which will possess all the pedagogical value of having religious education in the public schools without having it legally and formally there, as a natural, even inevitable, expedient. But when everything possible has been said for such plans, I still can't help noting four facts: (1) that they have not been conspicuously successful, from the standpoint either of the schools or of the churches; (2) that they always exist precariously, both legally and financially; (3) that they expose the churches to charges of sharp practice — always an uncomfortable situation for churches to find themselves in, however undeserved; (4) that the activities of such classes do not get down to what is the real issue, namely, the rescue of our culture from secularism. And I see that, both where such plans are in effect and where they are under consideration, a vast unhappiness persists among schoolmen and churchmen on both sides. Aside from those with a vested interest in extending or maintaining these marginal classes, no one seems satisfied. The characteristic defense, when defense is offered, explains: " Of course, this isn't very satisfactory, or what we want, or what we hope sometime to have. But at least it's a start, and given time . . ."

So here is our problem. Now let us look at it in more detail.

II

The secularization of Western culture has proceeded to a point where it is no longer honest to talk about "Christian nations," even in the loose sense in which that term was once employed. Western man is no longer at home in the Christian cultus. There was a time when, in Europe and the Americas, one could take for granted on the part of every literate person — and most illiterates — a background of Christian lore. That is no longer true. The one point on which chaplains serving the American forces during the recent war agreed was in what they regarded as the appalling religious ignorance of most of the men in the ranks. A generation or two generations ago any reference in a political speech or newspaper editorial to a passage from the Bible or to the principal Christian doctrines could be made without explanation, safe in the knowledge that it would be instantly understood. It is not so today. If a Theodore Roosevelt launches a Bull Moose campaign by shouting that "We stand at Armageddon," or if a Herbert Hoover warns against what will happen if the "four horse-men" ride across Europe, today's newspapers are careful to insert a paragraph of explanation to make the reference intel-ligible to their readers.* Authors still like to take their titles

* I once began a course of lectures on the relation of literature to preaching before an entering class in a theological seminary by holding a quiz in which the students were asked to identify fifty such quotations and allusions from biblical sources. All had been taken from recent books or speeches. None was of a particularly elusive nature. Not a member of the class was able to identify half the references.

Since I started to prepare this chapter for the press I noticed in the *Lutheran Witness* for Sept. 11, 1945, an amusing instance of the particular form of illiteracy here under discussion. This tells how a columnist in the *Detroit News* castigated Niemöller, the famous German pastor, for saying in a sermon that the gospel is "an offense to Jews and a stumbling-block to Greeks." After the word "Greeks" the columnist inserted in parentheses the words: "presumably the Greek Orthodox Church," and from the Bible — " The Voice of the Turtle," " Our Vines Have Tender Grapes," " A Lion Is in the Streets " — but that is because they hope thus, at one stroke, to give the effect of novelty to their output and to spread the idea that they are themselves persons of vast erudition who have searched crannies of ancient literature where few have ever penetrated before.

The problem for the churches is not simply that the majority of persons in Western countries today have no dynamic relationship with them (although that is unhappily true), but that the religious background which marked the culture of older generations has disappeared. All sorts of explanations are advanced to account for this state of affairs. Always among them will be included the disappearance of religious teaching from the public schools. The child in the lower schools, it is insisted, interprets the silence of the school on matters of religion and religious lore as meaning that, in the school's judgment, religion is a minor, even unnecessary, factor in the formation of our culture. And this " belittling " influence persists in our educational system right up through our colleges, so that our most distinguished historians, Charles and Mary Beard, can discuss *The Rise of American Civilization* in classic volumes which few college students fail to study with hardly a mention of the churches or of religion.

How did we get into this situation? Virtually all discussions of the problem begin with a review of the church origins of our colleges and lower school systems. Then they tell of the reasons why, in order to protect the public schools from the divisions and tensions caused by competing sectarian in-

---

then went on to explain that Niemöller was thus attacking modern Judaism and Greek Orthodoxy because they " do not accept divine teachings "! As the *Witness* remarks: " Quite evidently the columnist did not recognize one of the most familiar sayings of Paul." Yet he is accounted competent to pontificate to the readers of a distinguished American newspaper.

terests, the attitude of school neutrality or silence on matters of religion became general. From that they pass to the unsatisfactory nature of the alternative supplied by religious instruction in the Sunday school. I do not propose to go over that historical record again. If the reader wants to do so, let him consult almost any book dealing with the relation of religion to public education.* And I am not going to devote any space to the shortcomings of the Sunday schools. It is enough to note that, in the 5-to-17 age group, out of 31,618,000 young Americans the latest religious census (1936) showed less than 5,000,000 in Sunday schools. The decrease in the decade between 1926 and 1936 had been 40 per cent. Whether the youngsters who were enrolled were receiving anything approximating a grounding in religious truth and lore, I leave for the reader to answer.

But this whole record, so disastrous from the church's point of view, is really no more than a reflection of the changing nature of American life. Dr. Moehlman argues that we owe the disappearance of religious teaching from the public schools to the adoption of the First Amendment. If there was to be no establishment of religion, then there could be no particular interpretation of religion in the schools. But it was really the loss of homogeneity in our communities, rather than any constitutional or other legal enactments, which made the problem so difficult that the schools took refuge in a neutral silence. The kind of religious and moral teaching which was accepted without a question when our towns were made up, dominantly, of descendants of the original New England settlers, or of Scotch-Irish, or of Germans with a pietistic background (recall the McGuffey Readers!), became impossible after nearly every American community had become a melting-pot whose contents hadn't yet begun to melt. It was to make com-

* For example, *School and Church: The American Way*, by Conrad Henry Moehlman. New York: Harper & Brothers, 1944.

munity cohesion possible that religious education was ejected from the public schools.

III

A situation in which not more than a seventh of the American children of school age receive religious instruction in the Sunday schools, and in which more than a third of the states have constitutional provisions against such instruction in the public schools, cannot be satisfactory to the churches. Religious educators have long been predicting precisely the state of general religious illiteracy that the army and navy chaplains testify they have now encountered. The result has been the launching of various experiments designed to correct the secularistic character of public education.

The most important of these experiments has been the parochial school system, once tried by the Presbyterians, now conducted by certain Lutheran branches, but developed with the most determination by the Roman Catholics. In a famous encyclical on "Christian Education of Youth," Pius XI laid it down as a fundamental Catholic belief that "the so-called 'neutral' or 'lay' school, from which religion is excluded, is contrary to the fundamental purposes of education," and that "such a school . . . is bound to become irreligious." Therefore, the obligation is laid on Catholic parents not to send their children to non-Catholic (i.e., American public) schools, except in cases where there are no Catholic schools available and where the bishop gives his express approval. "Neither can Catholics," wrote the pope, "admit that other type of mixed school . . . in which the students are provided with separate religious instruction but receive other lessons in common with non-Catholic students."

What is to be said for the parochial school? As a theory of education which gives due weight to the importance of religious values, it is logically beyond attack. If the state insists upon secularistic education, for any prudential reasons which it may deem sufficient, then let the members of such communions as believe that education without religious instruction is lacking in an essential element erect their own schools, secure their own faculties, determine their own curricula and instruct their own children. Why not? The logical argument is sound. The legal position has been held by the United States Supreme Court, in its decision holding unconstitutional the Oregon law against parochial schools, to be equally sound. Why, then, isn't the parochial school the answer?

For many reasons. In the first place, it places an impossible financial burden on the members of the churches. The Presbyterians, who first tried the experiment on a large scale, had found that out before the Civil War. The Lutherans, despite an intense denominational loyalty which is rare in Protestant ranks, are able to induce their members to subject themselves to this form of double taxation only to the extent of providing parochial schools for 275,000 young Lutherans. Even the Catholics have never been able to get more than 43 per cent of their youth into parochial schools, though their people have been subjected to the most extreme kinds of pressure that priests and bishops can apply. In a nation with more than 35 million of school age the problem is just too large, and therefore too expensive, to be solved by a system of parochial schools. Catholic hopes that it can be brought within manageable limits by the appropriation of state funds for sectarian schools are, in American terms, I am convinced, doomed to disappointment. Certainly they should be.

Moreover, there is reason to believe that the parochial school tends to drive deep fissures through the community. It works against, not for, that process of amalgamation on which rests the future of such a country as this. The anonymous priest who wrote the oft-quoted article on " The Heresy of the Parochial School " which appeared in the *Atlantic Monthly* for

February 1928, stressed this shortcoming: " It is only by breaking the old associations and forming the new in good faith,
as we are, in fact, required to do by orthodoxy itself, that
Catholics can cease to be in this country an isolated foreign
colony, or a band of emigrants encamped for the night and
ready to strike their tents and take up their line of march on
the morrow for some other place." It is noticeable, also, that
the Lutheran congregations which cling most determinedly to
a parochial school system are mainly those which are at the
same time clinging to their " foreign " character and resisting
the fusing of their membership into the common American
amalgam.

If not the parochial school, then what? In 1913 Protestant
groups in the United States came forward with another proposal, that for the so-called " released time " plan of weekday
religious education. This plan takes various forms in various
states, depending somewhat on the limitations made necessary
by varying state laws, but its general aim is to provide a certain
amount of time, taken from the regular curriculum of the
public schools, in which pupils are allowed to attend classes
taught by teachers provided by the churches and synagogues.
Sometimes these classes are held in church buildings, sometimes
in the public school buildings. Sometimes they are taught by
clergymen, sometimes by trained lay teachers. It is of interest
to recall that the first experiment of this nature to gain national
attention was launched in one of the most heterogeneous communities in the United States — Gary, the Indiana steel city.
It is hardly too much to say that such released time classes
now constitute the white hope of the country's professional
religious educators. At last reports, about 1,800 American
communities, ranging in size from small villages to New York
city, had such classes.*

* For detailed outlines of the curriculum in many such classes, as well
as reports on the fortunes of the system as a whole, the reader may be re-

The released time system, it will be seen, attains the end of making possible the teaching of a certain amount of religious lore and perhaps even of catechetical material to pupils in public schools without actually being a part of the public school curriculum and without involving the use of tax money. Since the system is always voluntary, pupils attending or not as their parents elect, it cannot be objected to on grounds of religious freedom.   Why, then, has it not developed more rapidly?   Why do even those who support it frequently speak of it with such tempered enthusiasm?

There are many reasons.   It is sometimes objected that released time classes for religious instruction further subtract from the time available for regular instruction in public schools, where courses have already become such jumbled, atomized and helter-skelter affairs that no solid instruction can be given in anything.   As I write, for example, the newspapers in St. Louis are blaming released time classes in religious education for the poor showing in " three R " courses of students in the lower schools of that city.   Religious educators assert that the strictures of the newspapers reveal bias.   That may be so.   Yet the St. Louis papers have about as high a reputation for social responsibility as any group of papers in the country.   And their charge that released time classes in religion have been just the last straw that broke down the teaching effectiveness of the St. Louis school system has evidently awakened a public response.

Again, it is sometimes charged that a system of this sort, sending one group of pupils off to one church or classroom, another to another, and leaving still another not attending any of the classes, introduces invidious distinctions between pupils. In the mandamus proceedings to force the Champaign, Illinois, school board to suspend such classes, which attracted national

ferred to the bimonthly, *Religious Education*, published by the Religious Education Association, 20 West Jackson Blvd., Chicago 4, Ill.

attention when argued before the Illinois circuit court in September 1945, a charge of this sort proved to be one of the principal reliances of the plaintiffs. In other words, it is held that the released time plan is just as prolific of divisions in the community as would be an outright introduction of sectarian instruction in the school curriculum proper. Opponents of the plan who employ this argument tend to exaggerate the amount of division in the school body actually caused. But that a danger of this sort exists, there can be no doubt.

Still other criticisms of the system deal with the difficulty of finding teachers whose work will compare favorably with that of the teachers in the regular school courses, with the charge that this is actually a way of evading the provisions for separation of church and state without letting the unthinking portion of the community realize what is happening, with the contention that there are usually concealed drains on public funds involved, and with the most damaging allegation of all, namely, that students who go through such courses come out of them with no more grounding in religious knowledge than those who go through the much criticized Sunday schools. The released time system as it has worked so far, it is contended, has not made enough difference in the student's knowledge or character to make its continuation worth fighting for.

Is there, then, some alternate plan to bring forward? There is. It is the plan of which Dr. William Clayton Bower is probably the most distinguished champion among professional religious educators.* It would not have religion treated in the schools as a separate subject or discipline; religion, it insists, is integral to our total culture and should be treated in its relations to all the other elements in our culture. It would therefore have religion made a part of the regular subject matter of the schools. It believes that the released time programs fail

---

* Cf. *Church and State in Education,* by William Clayton Bower. Chicago: University of Chicago Press, 1944.

at the essential point of making religion integral to a comprehensive education; they still keep religion on the margin, where the psychological effect upon the student may not be as unfortunate as when religion is ignored altogether, but is nevertheless unfortunate. And when fears are expressed lest in this way sectarian divisions be introduced into the schools (Dr. Moehlman's book, which I have already mentioned, is mainly devoted to the energetic expression of such fears) then it is insisted that there is a " core " of religious knowledge, common alike to Catholic and Protestant, Christian and Jew, liberal and fundamentalist, which can be taught without any great danger of running into sectarian complications.

The most succinct and persuasive presentation of this view with which I am familiar was contained in a speech delivered first before the Missouri State Teachers Association in 1941 by Dr. Charles Clayton Morrison, and later published in the May 7 and 14 issues that year of the paper which Dr. Morrison edits, the *Christian Century*. In that speech, after a brilliant analysis of the problem, Dr. Morrison asked his teacher-audience to consider what he called " the most sensitive question in our democracy, namely, How can democracy grant religious freedom to its citizens and at the same time maintain a system of public education which includes religious instruction? " Dismissing the various experiments I have already mentioned as unsatisfactory, he proceeded to admit that sectarian rivalries had in the past forced religious education out of the public schools, yet contended:

It is my belief that we have come to a point where it is possible to transcend this sectarian rivalry which has inhibited religious instruction in public education. Two developments encourage this belief. One is the steady liberalization of the churches; the other is the development of an objective technique in education. By the liberalization of the churches I mean that the churches are increasingly coming to recognize that their sectarian differences are inconsequential as compared with the great body of truth which is the common denominator of their faith.

Insisting that " no one has a right to demand that his sectarian beliefs be taught in the public schools," the speaker then pointed out that this is just as true with regard to civics and economics and other subjects. Yet these are taught without doing violence to partisan prejudices, although our public schools contain the children of Democrats, Republicans, Socialists, Communists, capitalists, members of labor unions, and what not. It is no more impossible to " separate the common subject matter of religious faith from its sectarian variations " in order to make it the basis for public school instruction than it is to do so for the controversial subjects — most of them in the social sciences — already in the curriculum. Then, speaking directly to these teachers, Dr. Morrison made his plea:

You can show the churches and their clergy how this thing can be done. You can show them how you have developed a pedagogical technique that is competent to handle a religious subject matter with the same objectivity which characterizes your handling of all other subject matters. You can show these timid churchmen that it is possible for you to equip their children with a knowledge of the Bible and of religious history and of the actual forms which religion presents in their immediate community, and of the significance of religion in sustaining and enhancing democracy — you can show the churches that you can do all this without prejudice to the peculiarities of any particular sect. . . . There are countless local communities whose religious homogeneity is such that they would gladly open their schools to the experimentation which must necessarily precede the universal introduction of religious instruction into public education. When it is once demonstrated that religion can be taught in a manner acceptable to Catholic, Protestant and Jew, yes, and to that portion of the community which is not attached to any sect, the problem will be potentially solved.

Discussion evidently convinced the speaker that he had not made plain the sharp limits of the educational experiment which he had in view. At any rate, in later presentations of his thesis he insisted: " I am not in favor of transforming the school into a church. I do not advocate worship exercises with devotional Bible reading and prayer in the public school. Indeed, I oppose such an introduction of religion into the school system. We have every reason to be apprehensive when the state or secular community undertakes to direct the religious devotion of its youth. That way lies totalitarianism. But religious education and religious devotion are not the same; religious education is not religious evangelism. Religious education is the gaining of knowledge, true knowledge, *about* religion. . . . All we have the right to expect of the public school is that the educational process shall equip the student with the same kind of knowledge about religion as about any other subject in the curriculum."

This proposal deserves careful attention. I wonder, on reading it, whether there would be sufficient gain for the purposes in view by introducing religious instruction in classes thus specifically labeled " religion." More effective, I am inclined to believe, would be presentation of the body of material Dr. Morrison has in mind in connection with other classes, as for example in reading, in literature, in history or in almost any of the social sciences. And I question, likewise, whether this address has sufficiently taken into account the large amount of teaching in ethics, in morals, in religious history and in comparative religions which is already going on in the best of our public schools. But these are minor matters. The important thing is that we are presented with this picture of democracy crumbling at its core because of the failure of its schools to teach the faith on which it rests, and we are given this proposal whereby this process of inner disintegration may be stopped and our culture given a new moral orientation and vigor. Only considerations of the gravest importance should keep us from giving this proposal its chance to prove its claims in action.

Yet there are certain objections not to be lightly dismissed. First there are the objections of those who insist that it is not possible to do what Dr. Morrison calls for — to teach a " common subject matter of religious faith" — without becoming involved in sectarian disputes and producing community divisions. In arguing to this effect Dr. Moehlman tells the hypothetical story of a teacher who tries to present material as familiar as the Ten Commandments, the Twenty-third Psalm, the Lord's Prayer and the Beatitudes to a public school class only to become hopelessly entangled in sectarian differences in text and interpretation. Dr. Moehlman's hypothetical case rests too largely on the ineptness of a peculiarly resourceless teacher to be very convincing. But the problem he is trying to make concrete is a real one. Despite the assurance with which Dr. Morrison put it up to the Missouri teachers, I fear that any actual search for a generally acceptable " core " of instructional material regarding religion or a generally acceptable method of handling such material would disclose difficulties far more baffling than he has realized. Sad to say, there are after all definite limitations on the amount of " liberalization " which has taken place in a large number of American Protestant denominations, to say nothing of American Catholicism.

Again, it is objected by many who know the public school system well that the success or failure of this venture would depend on the cooperation of teachers who do not want to be burdened with the responsibilities for this added type of teaching, and who would therefore do it badly. This is not said to disparage the teachers. A certain proportion of them would undoubtedly welcome the opportunity to try experiments along this line. In most instances, these are the teachers who are already introducing into their own teaching far more serious presentation of ethical and moral truth than they frequently are given credit for doing. But the teaching profession, particularly in the lower schools, where the crux of this problem lies, is an underprepared and overworked livelihood, very few of whose members would be competent to undertake the sort of teaching now in consideration without extensive and expensive additional training. Naturally, such teachers would view the prospect of shouldering this added responsibility with hesitation and some dismay. The temptation would be great to discharge it with as little attention as would suffice to satisfy superintendents or boards of education.

Finally, and as far as I am concerned the most disquieting consideration of all, is the close similarity between this plan and that which has been in effect for decades in the schools of Germany, England, Holland and Scandinavia. Now, the results in these countries have not been all bad; one would not argue to that effect for a moment. But they certainly have not been all good. The formalism with which religion has been taught by bored or satirical or repellent schoolmasters in the public schools of Europe played its part in producing the formalism of the churches which made them so incapable of heading off the tragedy of two world wars in a generation. Neither do I think that it can be convincingly argued that the products of the European schools in which this sort of religious instruction has been required have been less overwhelmed by the secularistic tendencies of the age than the products of our American schools with all their " irreligiousness," as the pope calls it. And speaking of the pope, I do not believe that any comparison of the product of American schools with that of schools in countries where the Roman Church has a concordat-control of education will show less secularism in the outlook of the latter. If I could believe that, after its initial period of experimental adoption and careful supervision, this system which Dr. Morrison, Dr. Bower and those who support their

views propose would end in something essentially different
from that which has already been tried and found wanting
in Germany and England, I would be enthusiastically for it.
But I am not convinced that it would.

IV

There is one thing, however, against which we must be on
guard in all our consideration of the problem of religious instruction in relation to public education. Never for a moment
must we lose sight of the fact that the reason this problem has
become so exigent is that the faltering of democracy is hasten-
ing the rise of the omnipotent state, which is the totalitarian
state, which is Leviathan. It is the future of democracy, as
well as the freedom and strength of the church, which is at
stake here. For that reason, while we must never fail to submit
all proposals for action in this field to the most searching examination of which we are capable, we dare not rest content with
criticism and negation. Action of some sort is required. The
present crisis is too menacing, the religious foundations of our
faith in democracy are crumbling too rapidly, for us to be willing that public education should go on unchanged. What is to
be done?

For my part, I do not see that any single proposal now before
us can meet the requirements of this situation. But accepting
without reservation the wisdom of the principle of separation
of church and state, and of the prohibition against the use of
public funds for sectarian purposes, I still think that certain
steps can be taken to erect barriers against the further penetra-
tion of the totalitarian philosophy into our American life.
Some of these steps will need to be experimental; we will take
them tentatively. Others, as will presently appear, are as yet
so far from clear to me that I am not sure precisely what the
steps should be — only that they should be in the direction
indicated. I do not present this, therefore, as a complete or

final program. It is no more than a collection of suggestions for action in a time when action of some kind is urgently demanded. But it is enough to keep our consideration of this aspect of the problem of the future of church and state from ending on a note of frustration.

First, then, I believe that schoolmen should take the lead in pointing out to our American communities that there is a certain cultural heritage of religion which should be in the curriculum of our schools. Without it, not only will the schools continue to present a one-sided interpretation of our culture, from which essential elements are lacking, but they will fail to make clear to young Americans the philosophic basis for our faith in democracy and the dynamic which has made that a living political and social order. Our schoolmen can begin at once to bring this part of our cultural heritage back into the schools. I believe that they will find it easier to do this, and that the results will be more satisfying, if it is done as part of the now familiar courses, rather than by adding to the curriculum new classes in a special discipline labeled " religion."

I believe, in the second place, that the various forms of so-called " released time " classes constitute an experiment which should be continued. So much effort has already been put into these classes by the churches and by educators, and so many communities have been won to a friendly interest in what is being attempted, that it would be foolish to toss the whole venture into the discard at this stage. However, I believe that the future will be best served if not too much is looked for from these experiments. The hindrances which lie in their way as they attempt to reach what must be, at least in theory, their goal — bringing education in religion to the almost thirty million young Americans who receive no such education in parochial or Sunday schools — are so insurmountable that they can hardly hope to be more than an auxiliary aid, and not a very strong one at that. Moreover, their position on the margin of our educational system, placed there of their own choice, is bound to limit these released time classes in religion to a marginal influence.

In the third place, I trust that the Roman Catholic and Lutheran parochial schools will continue. If they are able to increase their enrollment, I will have no objection. If there is a place for the church-related college in the American educational system (and I believe with the overwhelming majority of my fellow Protestants that there is) then there seems no reason to deny that there may be a place for the church-related high school and grammar school. The only safeguards that need to be insisted on are (1) that the parochial schools shall maintain as high pedagogical and scholarship standards as are maintained in the public schools; (2) that there shall be as much care exercised in seeing that the students are grounded in the other aspects of the American tradition as in the contributions of religion; (3) that such schools shall be supported entirely by private funds, and conversely (4) that prohibitions against the use of public funds, either directly or indirectly, in the support of such schools shall be honestly and rigidly observed.

Fourth, I believe that there is no reason to despair of what our better schools and teachers are already doing in familiarizing their pupils with the great truths and facts of the Christian heritage, and because there is no such reason, it behooves Christian ministers and lay leaders to become more familiar with what is actually taking place in these better classrooms in order that they may give intelligent encouragement to the educators who have already tackled this task. Dr. Bower tells of a recent survey of elementary classrooms made by Professor Ernest J. Chave, which disclosed ten categories of essentially religious values continually stressed: " A sense of the worth of persons, development of social sensitivity, growth in appreciation of the universe, growth in the discrimination of values,

growth in the sense of responsibility and accountability, recognition of the need for cooperative fellowship, recognition that the quest for truth and the realization of ideals is a slow and endless pursuit, development of a working philosophy of life, observance of special times and ceremonies, and development of adequate means of expression of spiritual values and goals." *
One trouble has been that certain religious observers are so traditionally minded that they fail to perceive the important religious content of such teaching. They insist on the label, " This, children, is religion "; or even, " This, children, is Christianity." What we really need, I believe, is recognition of the large amount of essentially religious teaching that is already going on in our public schools, encouragement for the teachers who are giving it, and a mission to teachers to awaken in them a sense of Christian responsibility to undertake the same sort of teaching. Most of them are already in the churches, where it should be a simple matter to confront them with the importance of their task and to start them seeking ways to discharge it in a spirit of religious consecration.

Fifth, what I have just said will suggest that I believe that most of the teaching of the " lore " of Christianity and of distinctive Christian (or Jewish) doctrine is the responsibility of the church and must be done by the church. I do not believe that it can be made a responsibility of the public school without producing community tensions and fissures more costly to the democratic future than any gains which might thus be sought. How, it will be asked, is the church to discharge this responsibility? I do not know. Its present educational program is so limited that there is no reason to hope for much from it. But I have a hunch (if the expression annoys the reader I am sorry, but I use it because it is the correct one — I am not sure; I simply have a hunch) that the churches can do this by moving in two directions: first, by making their

* Bower, *op. cit.*, p. 66.

present program of activities much more educational in character; and second, by accepting a new responsibility for the education of the adults in their membership. Aside altogether from what could be done to give more educational content to worship services, if the churches would once begin to use the innumerable meetings of committees, boards, guilds, clubs, circles and whatnot that now crowd their calendars to do some genuine teaching in Christian doctrine, history and ethics, that would probably work as quickly as any method could to wipe out the stigma of religious illiteracy. And if they would acknowledge a responsibility for the religious education of parents, as well as of the children the parents send off to Sunday school once a week, that too might make a decided and speedy difference. At any rate, I am convinced that here is the logical point at which to start some new experiments.

Sixth (and what I have to say from this point on constitutes negative, but nonetheless important, suggestions), in all that we undertake to insure democracy's religious undergirding we must allow no doubts to arise as to our devotion, as churchmen, to the principle of separation of church and state. Too much history is involved to play fast and loose with that now. Strangely enough, despite persistent papal condemnations of the principle, there have been numbers of unafraid Roman Catholics who have testified that the church itself has gained in spiritual strength in all the countries where the principle has been observed. Nothing that we do when experimenting in this field should be permitted to give any observer the idea that we are trying to find some " slick " formula whereby we give lip service to this principle while actually managing to circumvent it.

Another word of warning constitutes the seventh suggestion I would underscore. Whatever forms our experimentation may take, let us have no confusion as to the fact that nothing will be gained by trying to *force* religious teaching into our public schools. The task we face is a task for reason and persuasion — and nothing more! Efforts to force the pace will defeat their own ends. Until the community is sure that it wants to have religion a part of the education of its children — and that not by any narrow margin — there is no justification in moving. It was at this point that Dr. Charles Clayton Morrison, in the proposals to which I have already referred, showed his greatest wisdom. He made his approach to the teachers, suggesting that they demand as a necessity for undergirding democracy changes in the school curriculum along the lines he outlined. He knew better than to call for church pressure groups to force such an experiment over on a doubting and reluctant public. Instead, he turned to the one group which could most persuasively take up the task of convincing public opinion.

Finally, there is a certain amount of opposition for which we must always be prepared. I am not now thinking of local opposition from individuals and local groups. This, as I have just said, must be dealt with on a level of reason and persuasion. But there is an opposition of a different sort; an opposition from major political forces and interests which is likely to take form the moment it is clear that the sort of general education the churches seek is a threat to the pretensions of expanding state power. To the very extent to which the churches try to introduce basic religious beliefs into the curriculum of the public school — such beliefs as the supremacy of the moral law, the inviolability of conscience, the oneness of mankind, the equal worth of all human beings, the inviolability of personality — the state, as it seeks Leviathan status, will resist such infiltration. When this opposition is encountered, the requirement is not for sweet reasonableness, patience and delay. When this opposition is encountered, the church must give and accept no truce. For the conception of education which the church champions must be incorporated in the nation's schools, lest the nation's people shall presently discover that the Leviathan state has used a secularistic educational system to betray them into a totalitarian slavery.

CHAPTER X

LEVIATHAN WITH A FISH-HOOK

I

" Canst thou draw out Leviathan with a fish-hook? " the
Lord demanded of Job. " Canst thou put a rope through his
nose? Or pierce his jaw through with a hook? Upon earth
there is not his like. Everything that is high fears him. He
is king over all the sons of pride."

This ancient challenge flung into the face of the abashed
Job takes on new meaning as we confront our modern Leviathan, the totalitarian state. Have we any fish-hooks, any ropes
by which we can control him? Or is this Leviathan still too
strong for puny man to harness? This, said Abraham Lincoln,
is the perennial problem of government: " Must a government,
of necessity, be too strong for the liberties of its own people,
or too weak to maintain its own existence? " The pressures
today driving governments toward accumulating ever greater
powers are ceaseless and all but intolerable. Can the liberties
of the people survive in a world of this sort?

In recent years there has been a significant change in the discussion of revolutionary possibilities and techniques that is
always going on in extreme radical circles. The emphasis
today is all upon the almost insuperable difficulties faced by
revolutionaries. A century, even a few decades, ago, we are
told, revolution was a relatively simple matter. Let the people
be sufficiently aroused to throw off their allegiance to the established government, smuggle firearms to a portion of the
populace, call the mob into the streets to throw up barricades

217

and hurl cobblestones at the legs of the troopers' horses, and
lo, the revolution! That pattern repeated itself so frequently
in nineteenth century Europe that it became all but standard-
ized.

But today? Ah, today the case is changed. Napoleon's
" whiff of grapeshot " has grown to the blasting military power
possessed by all strong governments. The barricades offer no
problem to tanks. The mobs in the streets will not stay there
long after a strafing or bombing airplane appears overhead. A
thousand rifles in the hands of untrained marksmen may not
suffice to silence a single machine gun. This is not to say that
revolution has become entirely impossible in the modern state.
The brooding would-be revolutionist still reads Trotsky's
lessons in how to render a modern capital helpless, no matter
how well equipped and disciplined the government forces.
But it is true that uprising against the entrenched state has
become infinitely more difficult, and perilous, than it was a
few generations ago. With the prospect that the state may
soon have atomic power under its control to use for purposes
of defense, the way of the revolutionist becomes all but impossible. What fish-hooks have we by which to catch our
modern Leviathan? What ropes by which to drag him safely
to land?

II

In the pages which have gone before I have been trying, all
too inadequately, to suggest how swiftly this issue of the
power of an omnicompetent state has become a matter of life
and death for men's liberties and for the liberty of the Christian church. I have been trying to point out that, while the
problem of relationship between state and church is an old
problem, and one never solved, it is upon us in these days in a
form and with a threat never surpassed, if equaled, in danger.
I noticed an illuminating proof of the newness of our problem

when I read again the most recent of the Earl Lectures to deal
with this state and church issue. That was the distinguished
series of lectures delivered by Dr. S. Parkes Cadman and published by the Macmillan Company in 1924 under the title,
Christianity and the State. Naturally, in daring to revert to
the same topic so soon in the same lectureship, I felt it necessary to examine again what my predecessor had said. And in
doing so I found that, as recently as 1924, Dr. Cadman had
apparently never heard of the term " totalitarianism," and that
he found it quite possible to discuss the relations of the church
with government without ever referring to the pretensions of
a " totalitarian state." Though an old problem, it is upon us
now, I repeat, in a new form.

I have been trying likewise, in the pages which have gone
before, to show that the progress of modern states toward
totalitarian forms of organization and control has not been
ended by the recent war. On the contrary, the war has left
a pervasive instability throughout the world which encour-
ages the growth of totalitarianism. The drift toward seeking
individual security in the omnicompetent state is as marked in
the Western democracies as in the states which are avowedly
moving toward a collectivist order, and are trying to evade the
issue of personal freedom by insisting that there must be new
definitions for such words as freedom, liberty and democracy.
Expanded definitions, they are called. The old definitions
were too narrow. Perhaps so, but on examination it will be
found that the " expansion " in the new all but succeeds in
wiping out the old definition altogether. The power of Soviet
Russia, great victor in the war, most tightly organized of all
totalitarian states, constitutes an element in this present trend
toward the increase of state power which cannot be left
out of account. With such a world as this left by the war, few
will even seriously try to argue that the ignominious end of
Hitler or of Mussolini or of the Japanese war lords has greatly

retarded, much less ended, the trend toward the omnipotent state.

Yet along with the apprehension which this book has thus tried to reflect and explain, there goes an equally profound belief in the importance of the Christian church.* I have tried to approach the question of the nature of the modern state from this angle of the church because of my conviction that the church remains one of the principal instrumentalities, perhaps *the* principal instrumentality, by which the freedom of man is to be defended. Yes, I know, Thomas à Becket's body lies moldering on Canterbury's altar steps, but his soul goes marching on. And the need for such a book as this on this often-explored subject lies, it seems to me, in the fact that so few Christian churchmen in the democratic countries are awake to the desperate nature of the impending struggle or how soon, if the church does its duty by harassed man, it may break in full fury.

The totalitarian Leviathan is with us and growing, I have tried to make clear, not because men want tyranny. But men want safety. Hardly a handful of men, even in our proud and rich America, feel safe any more. It is not only safety for themselves that they seek. Much more characteristically it is safety for their homes, their children's future. Where has such safety vanished? When the economic and political problems that lie ahead come to seem more and more difficult of solution — as they will — more and more such frightened men will come to regard the power of the state as their last hope.

How large a part of the population of the United States is already dependent for a considerable proportion of its liveli-

* Here, and almost everywhere throughout the text, the reader may add the words, " and Jewish synagogue." I have not done so because I did not want to make the text too cumbersome. But it is the institution which exists as the receptacle and renewer of the Judeo-Christian heritage that I have in mind throughout.

hood on subsidies, direct or indirect, or on direct payroll checks from the government? I do not know, but I believe that any honest examination of that question would yield astonishing results. Why, even some of our most rugged individualists, who insist most loudly on the iniquity of all kinds of government aid for the unemployed, insist with equal vehemence on the maintenance of systems of export subsidies which are nothing less than a government handout to enable them to defy natural economic law. If, after our first post-victory boom has flattened out, as it will, we are confronted by the threat of mass unemployment and consequent social catastrophe, the demand for a huge and inclusive program of government planning will become too strong to be denied.

I am not condemning planning. Anyone can see that we could well have done with more of it in the past than we have had. Nevertheless, it does no good to shut our eyes to the fact that the successful operation of a program of government-planned production and distribution requires a constant accumulation of power by the government. Why? For the obvious reason that when the government's program runs into difficulties — something it is bound to do, since human beings cannot be counted on always to react to new regulations as the authors of those regulations have expected, as any of the authors of our wartime OPA and WFA regulations can testify — when the government's program runs into difficulties, then there is no choice before the government, short of abandoning its plan, but to seek new powers to deal with the new hindrances. We saw that again and again during the war. And powers once acquired are never surrendered without a severe struggle.

But this gradual accumulation of power in the hands of governmental authority moves us ever closer to the reality of a totalitarian order, even though here in America we can be counted on never to call it by that name. The late Huey

Long's wisecrack bearing on this has been so often quoted that
it is threadbare. However, I quote it again because, threadbare or not, it contains a true observation on the American
character. Huey Long, the Louisiana führer, said that if fascism ever comes to America we will call it anti-fascism. Similarly, if totalitarianism comes we can be counted on to call it
democracy or the New Liberty or something equally be-
guiling.

At all costs the freedom of man must be preserved. Not
man simply as an atom in the structure of a monolithic society,
but man as an individual, man as man. Here is where the
church comes in. The church is the only institution we have
that knows beyond all argument *why* man as an individual
must be free. That has just been proved by the contrast between the defiance of the church and the abdication of education and science in the presence of Hitler. If I have the
slightest understanding of the Christian gospel, this lies at its
very foundation. I believe in the freedom of man because
I believe in the God revealed by Jesus Christ. While I cherish
that belief I, and all churchmen with me who know why they
are churchmen, must steady the church to defend the freedom
of man against the encroaching powers of the state. Here we
stand. God help us, we can do no other.

III

One legitimate objection, I am aware, may be made to the
presentation of the menace of the Leviathan state in the foregoing pages. Too frequently, I have referred to the state as
though it were, like Karl Barth's deity, something " wholly
other," something not only apart from the citizen but over
against, in opposition to, in unrelieved tension with, the citizen. The state is made to appear an ogre outside the citizen's
life, who invades that life, captures it and finally controls it
from afar as an alien conqueror.

This, of course, is a travesty. At least in the nations which still cling to democratic forms, the state is not something apart but the sum of the political wills of its citizens. If the state is a tyrant, it is not a tyrant who has invaded from some alien world, but a tyrant I have myself formed (working in concert with my fellow citizens), whose chains I have myself forged and fastened. Certainly this is the claim of democracy.

To go far into the issue which this objection raises would require a study of the nature of the state, particularly of the modern state. How far do its constitutional constructs agree with its realities? How far does it exist as its myth asserts, and how far is it something that is never acknowledged, either in law or tradition? The issue is too big to be crowded into such a book as this. Here I cannot do more than assert that, as the state grows in size and complexity, it escapes more and more from any genuine democratic controls. As its administrative bureaucracy proliferates, the process of administration takes on more and more a life of its own, with its own vested interests, which sets it off by itself, apart from the citizens, indeed over the citizens.

It will be asserted that there still remain in a democracy means for bringing this self-perpetuating and self-ordering state back under the control of the citizen. There do. This is one of the remaining hopeful elements in the situation. But because these exist, in theory and even in law, let no one think that it will prove easy to make them work in practice. There is nothing automatic about them — less so than ever now that the perils of the atomic age will create a demand for fast action on the state's part: " Survival depends on getting in the first blow! "

A study of recent American history will show that, dating from the rise of Populism, the major effort of " democrats " has been to find ways by which to re-establish this sort of citizen's control over a state that was getting increasingly out of hand. All sorts of expedients have been tried, each presented in its turn as a sovereign remedy for all our ills. The Australian ballot, universal suffrage, initiative, referendum, recall, direct primaries, direct election of senators, public ownership, income tax — the list is only partial, but it is long enough to suggest the many varying ways in which a growingly complex country has tried to restore popular control of government and responsiveness by the state to the popular will. One need not be a fascist to admit the limited nature of the results achieved.

When it is said that all this record proves is that " eternal vigilance is the price of liberty " and that we must never cease to struggle to make the state democratic in fact as well as in assumption, I agree. But let us not deceive ourselves as to the actual state of affairs today. It is with this actual state of affairs that this book has been trying to deal. The state — even the avowedly democratic state — today *does* exist almost apart from the life of the citizen. It makes demands on him; he goes to it for favors (they may be no more than to have the garbage carted away from the alley behind his residence, but it is nevertheless a suppliant's plea he makes) or throws himself upon it for succor. Yet never, or seldom ever, does he think of himself as the state's maker or the state's master.

Even the highly educated technician or administrator who goes into state service tends to absorb this same conception of the state as something apart. To him it becomes a mechanism, a power that operates on people; not something of the people. He feels that there is rewarding satisfaction in being able to take the state machinery and apply it to the lives of the people in order to see what it can accomplish. It is gigantic machinery, and manipulating it gives the administrator or technician the thrill of using great power. But that

is not the way by which there will be restored to the citizen
a vital sense of the reality of his sovereignty.   On the contrary, that is one way by which his sense of helplessness, his
sense of being a pawn, is increased.

IV

We are entering, I am convinced, upon a period of great
fear.   It seems a betrayal of our dead to say this as we emerge
from a war which was being fought, we were assured, to free
all men from fear.   Have the millions who laid down their
lives died in vain?   If they died with any idea that fear was
thereby to be banished from the earth, they have.   Fear has
not been banished.   There would even be many to dispute any
claim that there is less fear today, in this hour of victory, than
there was in the black years before Hitler flung down the final
gage of battle.

Nothing, I presume, makes us more aware of the perilous
nature of these days than the fact that victory in the war
brought us so little of a sense of exultation.   What thoughtful
mind could listen to the speeches which greeted our triumph,
to the radio programs, or read the words of the professional
word-mongers without detecting the synthetic quality of our
rejoicing?   The plain truth was that we were not exultant,
and no matter how often we told ourselves that we should be,
no matter how hard we tried, we could not be.   The war had
brought us no security, and we knew it.   Now we listen in
amazement to the admirals and the generals as they troop back
to Congress demanding great fleets, great armies, a great network of " security " bases.   Can they really believe that there
is security in such things?   Or do their tongues run on because, having become accustomed to make such sounds, they
can think of nothing else to do in this awful hour?

There is no security for us.   We live in the world of the
atom bomb.   Witless as is the demand for more battleships,

is it a whit more so than the frenzied conferences to discuss the " control " of this new force, or the rush of legislators as I write to introduce bills to render us secure from this new agent of destruction? How can you control a scientific discovery of that sort short of building a society in which men live in such contentment that they will have no desire to resort to its use for purposes of devastation? And how far have we to go before we will have built such a world society?

Our economic future is as dark as our political and military future. The air is full of debate concerning loans, tariffs, commodity exchanges, inflation and deflation and the respective rights of labor and investment. What will happen if we cancel? Or if we don't cancel? What will happen if we grant? Or if we don't grant? Our advisers differ hopelessly among themselves. Meanwhile we, the common people, know only that there are tens of millions homeless in the world today, hundreds of millions hungry or facing the prospect of hunger. If we snatch at such measures of self-protection as seem available to us today, we have a haunting fear lest these may be the very means of bringing on a world economic collapse that will overwhelm us tomorrow.

Then to add to all our fears, in some ways the most destructive of all our fears, is the suspicion that grows within us that our leaders are not capable of coping with this world. They seem to know no more than we, the common people, know. They have no greater wisdom than we have. We are puny, frightened men, in the hands of puny, frightened men. Look about the earth today and what is the spectacle you see? Little men with little minds throwing little words up against gigantic problems.

v

Has the Christian church anything to offer us in our dire extremity? If I did not believe that it had, I would not be writing. I believe that the church has a tremendous responsibility to discharge lest, in this hour of our bewilderment and fear, we supinely surrender ourselves and man's destiny into the hands of Leviathan.

First, there is needed renewed appreciation of the importance of the fact that the church exists to proclaim the nature and the will of the Christian God. This comes before everything else. This it must do unceasingly. And in doing this the church will make its greatest contribution to the undergirding of democracy and the subduing of Leviathan. It is good to see the church, after a period of distraction caused by its sudden realization of the unchristian nature of Western society, getting back to this first principle and beginning again to put its primary emphasis here where it belongs.

The return to theology on the part of the church is not a retreat from the battle. It is an advance toward the heart of the battle. Who is this God whom we say we worship, and what does he require of man? What is the nature and worth of this man to whom God stretches forth his hand in redemption? These are the concerns upon which the church must first satisfy itself and fix its mind. These are the first things that must be kept first. For if the church does not know what it believes, how can it know where its faith is threatened? How can it know what to fight for, and what to fight against?

Second, the church has a responsibility as never before to keep itself free from any form of state subsidy or control. Too often in the past we have tried to play fast and loose with this issue, to eat our cake and have it. We have been too ready to lean on the secular arm, without realizing that the secular arm was encircling the church and throttling it. This, it may be asked, relates to the question of state churches? It does. Nothing that a church can conceivably gain by making itself an organ or an adjunct of a state will recompense it for the jeopardy in which it places its prophetic liberty. As I write I see no more pathetic blindness among those who would struggle against Leviathan than the attempt on the part of the rescued and revived Evangelical Church of Germany to obtain some continued form of state support. Why do the devoted men and women of that communion, who have learned such bitter lessons in these past dozen years, close their eyes to *this* lesson — that the church cannot exist on the bounty of Caesar without becoming the victim of Caesar?

But the issue goes beyond that of state churches. It relates to other matters, such as, for example, the exemption of churches and their property from taxation; the use of state funds — perhaps I should say the *pursuit* of state funds — for the support of many kinds of church enterprises; the support of chaplains for the men in the armed forces and for inmates of state institutions by the state and their commissioning by the state. The issue even existed, during the recent war, in the status of camps for conscientious objectors, and their administration by the churches as an arm of the state. And it now exists, I am informed, in the decision of certain mission boards to accept " cultural relations " funds from the United States government to expand their missionary work in the Near East and India.

It is amazing that experienced church mission board executives should not see the false position in which any Christian work financed by the funds of a foreign government will always stand. The fact that they have not, but have eagerly accepted the money which Mr. Nelson Rockefeller and his successors in the U. S. state department have offered, is only another demonstration that we have been far too blind to the numerous ways by which, in an effort to lighten the burden of carrying on the proper work of the church, we have been willing to rest back on the support of the state. We must begin to extricate the church at once from this false position, and with a new determination, for as long as it persists the church's freedom to proclaim judgment is compromised.

Will this involve a curtailment of the church's activities or a contraction of its physical equipment? It is possible. And it is equally possible that the church can do its essential work, proclaiming the truth of its gospel and holding state and society up to judgment, more powerfully with fewer million-dollar institutions and " seven-day " programs. Nothing will more surely make the masses suspect the independence and good faith of the church than to know that it is under obligation in keeping its property and enterprises intact to some element which stands to profit from preservation of the status quo.

In the past this suspicion, as churchmen are only too unhappily aware, has been directed against the allegedly disproportionate influence in church affairs exercised by wealthy laymen and the " big business " point of view. In the future, however, as the state gathers power and uses it with increasing determination and decreasing popular control, suspicion of the freedom of the church to discharge its prophetic function as the conscience of the state will certainly grow if the church is known to be dependent on state favors. A tax exemption, a draft exemption, a subsidy for school or hospital or asylum or mission station can cost a tragic price in public confidence.

Third, the time has come for the church to proclaim the end of the world of nationalism and the necessity for the transformation of our existing national loyalties into a globe-encircling loyalty to one world state. I know that violent dissent will greet that statement, but at this dawn of the atomic age I do not see what other position the church can take. Am I talking about a super-government? I am not. The thing I am talking about is a true and inclusive world government which shall not transcend or outrank but which shall supersede and absorb the competing sovereignties which have brought us to our present crisis. Tennyson prophesied a " federation of the world." That prophecy has never entirely been forgotten. Even President Truman has exhibited the frayed clipping of " Locksley Hall " he has carried in his wallet for years.

But a federation of states is not enough. A federation implies something less than complete union; something which sovereign states enter at their own desire and withdraw from at their own pleasure. That is not the goal to which the Christian church must point mankind now — not in this atomic age. Many of us, perhaps almost all of us, agreed with Chancellor Hutchins of the University of Chicago when he said, the week after the destruction of Nagasaki, that while he had not heretofore believed that mankind's thought had reached the stage where it is ready seriously to consider the idea of a world state, the control of atomic energy confronts us with a problem so insoluble in nationalistic terms that the world state idea must now be accepted in principle. To the church falls the responsibility not only of fostering the idea in principle but rousing the will of the peoples to move toward the goal.

Nor is there any time to be lost. It will seem utterly foolish to some to talk about moving decisively toward any such goal as a world state now. " Oh yes, sometime," they will concede, like indulgent parents trying to humor an unreasonable child. " But that is something in the far, far distant future — five hundred years from now, says Mortimer Adler; more likely a thousand, or five thousand. Now we must be realistic. Now we must reckon with men as they are, and with all the traditions and the loyalties which are so deeply embedded in their consciousness. Slowly, cautiously, not forcing the pace, not frightening the mind with unaccustomed ideas, we can suggest little steps that will begin to point the nations toward a new goal. But not all at once; not in a hurry; not now. Haste makes waste."

That must not be the voice of the church. One of the tragic but inescapable elements in our present crisis is our lack of time. Always in the past the church, in the background of its thinking, has taken comfort in a sense of its illimitable time vistas. A thousand years has been as a day; the church has believed that it had all the millenniums in which to induce man to work out the purposes of the Almighty. It is so no longer. We no longer have the millenniums. We have a few brief years — how few and how fleeting the mind can scarcely bear to contemplate. Destruction threatens, not at the end of a long road, but within the life span of boys and girls now living. Haste may make waste, but delay will bring desolation.

Perhaps history will affirm that the atomic bomb has been a terrifying experience that we needed to open our eyes to the fact that the age of nationalism had already reached its end. For it is only in two nations — the U.S.A. and the U.S.S.R. — that the idea of unrestricted national sovereignty has the slightest chance of maintaining its authority much longer. Even in these mighty states there are distinct limitations on the extent to which the national will can be exerted without reference to the wills or welfare of the rest of mankind. Yet it is true that these states are strong enough, nearly enough self-sufficient so that they can, if they choose, cling to an autarchy which their people may be deceived for a time into believing will provide both security and abundance.

Yet it is only in the case of these two giant nations that any belief in the future of national self-sufficiency can survive. The other nations already know that their fate is wrapped up in the fate of others. It will not be long before they will see that persistence in dividing the world into separate parts, separate interests, separate cliques can only mean persistence in fomenting the discord that will ultimately produce conflict. Then the fall of the bomb — and lights out!

With this responsibility resting upon it to proclaim the necessity for a true union of mankind in one state, the Christian church should rejoice in the providential preparation which has placed a new emphasis on its own ecumenicity. It may well be that the most direct way in which to bear witness to the need for unity among the peoples is by demonstrating a world-wide unity among the churches. Certainly everything that savors of clinging to old denominational sovereignties and sectarian factionalisms is a hindrance to any effective proclamation of the goal of a world state. The cry is, " Unite or die," and it applies to the churches as much as to the nations.

Finally, I believe that the time has come when the church must take with new seriousness its responsibility to act as monitor to the state concerning the requirements of the moral law. Here most of all is the point at which the church needs to recapture its prophetic fire and its prophetic significance. I use the terms with hesitation, for they have become part of that vocabulary of pious exhortation which churchmen toss about so constantly and with so little meaning. Little is to be gained by exhorting the church to regain its prophetic function. The fire of true prophecy will begin to burn again only when the church awakens to a realization that it is involved in such a crisis as threatens its whole future. Prophecy arises out of crisis; out of what some Continental theologians speak of as a " divine confrontation." The crisis can be counted on to follow if ever the church tells the state that it must obey the moral law — provided, of course, that it does so in such a way that the state, with its insatiable itch after power, knows that the church means what it says.

One of the factors which kept the Chinese Empire alive longer than any other empire in history was the institution known as the censor. The censor was a man of unimpeachable character and tested moral insight who at any time had immediate access to the person of the emperor, in order to warn that absolute monarch of any wanderings from the line of conduct laid down by China's sages. That, one knows as one recalls Nathan before David, Elijah before Ahab, Jeremiah before Jehoiakim, Amos before the tawdry court and priesthood at Bethel, was also the role of the Hebrew prophets. And that must be the role of the Christian church in its relations with the modern state. It has, to its glory, been the role of much of the church in the presence of many of the totalitarian tyrannies which have overrun Europe in recent years. It must become its role everywhere so long as the trend toward concentration of power in the hands of the state continues.

So I close where I began, with Thomas Hobbes and his Leviathan, the state — " that mortal God to which we owe our peace and our defense." For the Christian church, while time lasts, there can be no truce with any mortal God.

LINCOLN CHRISTIAN COLLEGE AND SEMINARY 116406

261.7
H977

3 4711 00188 2069